JOHN McGRATH

# The Bone Won't Break

## *On Theatre and Hope in Hard Times*

METHUEN DRAMA

A METHUEN PAPERBACK

First published in Great Britain in 1990 by Methuen Drama,
Michelin House, 81 Fulham Road, London SW3 6RB and distributed
in the United States of America by HEB Inc, 70 Court Street,
Portsmouth, New Hampshire 03801.

A CIP catalogue record for this book
is available from the British Library.
ISBN 0 413 63260 1

Typeset in 11/12½pt Linotron Plantin by
Hewer Text Composition Services, Edinburgh
Printed and bound in Great Britain by
Cox & Wyman Ltd, Cardiff Road, Reading

The painting on the front cover is *The Red Flag*, in pastel
and gouache, © John Howson, Angela Flowers Gallery.
The photograph on the back cover is of John McGrath and
the Nissan car workers in New Zealand, where the workers
went on strike against the Nissan company culture. © New
Zealand Herald, 1988.

CAUTION

# The Bone Won't Break

This title comes from a particular version of the children's game
*The Farmer's In His Den* played in Edinburgh.

In it, as in all versions, the 'Farmer' stands in the middle of
the ring, and the others circle round him or her chanting the
verse, until he or she has to choose his Wife, who then joins him
or her in the ring, and in turn, chooses the Child, who also joins
them. And so on until the Dog, who chooses a Bone – usually the
most put-upon child in the group, who then has to stand in the
middle while the others go round singing We all pat the Bone,
and hitting the poor bone, who tries to dodge the blows. The
Bone stays there, then they all sing The Bone Won't Break!

There is a different version on Merseyside, where the last
event is the singing of We All Lift The Bone – and the child in
the middle is hoisted up and dropped, then hoisted up in the air
again. Maybe this is more optimistic in its view of human
nature. I'm not sure. They do drop them a bit hard.

Here are the words.

> The Farmer's in his den.
> The Farmer's in his den.
> Ee aye my daddy-oh,
> The Farmer's in his den.
>
> The Farmer wants a Wife, etc
>
> The Wife wants a Child, etc
>
> The Child wants a Nurse, etc
>
> The Nurse wants a Dog, etc
>
> The Dog wants a Bone, etc
>
> We all pat the Bone, etc
>
> The Bone won't break,
> The Bone won't break,
> Ee aye my daddy-oh,
> The Bone won't break . . .

# CONTENTS

# PREFACE

The six pieces which follow were first given as a series of weekly talks to a group of undergraduates and graduates at Cambridge University, in the English Faculty, between October and December 1988. It was a very particular audience, and the timing had a certain significance. Just about ten years before, between January and March 1979, I had given, to a similar audience in Cambridge, the six accounts of my theatre work and aspirations which were published as *A Good Night Out*.

Within three months of my giving those talks, the first Thatcher government came to power. Few of us then would have believed just what they and their successors were capable of, what cultural terrorism they engaged in during the whole of the 80s. The source of funding and guidance for most of the new theatre work of the 70s, the Arts Council, was gutted from top to bottom, and left, gutless, in the life-extinguishing grip of the then Sir William Rees-Mogg. The whole blossoming bough of popular theatre, which was all set to achieve so much for British theatre, was clumsily hacked off. Ideological repression and fiscal misery combined to change the geography of the arts.

As I was invited, at fairly short notice, to go back to Cambridge for another spell, I accepted in the hope of being able to come to grips with the experience of those intervening ten years. I was, of course, keen to chart my own shatteringly archetypal adventures in some hopefully illuminating detail, as a modest contribution to the social history of British theatre in the 80s. I wanted also to set these comparatively well-cushioned blows in the wider context of the deprivation, suffering – mental and physical – and immiseration of so many people in certain sections of society during those grimly reactionary years. I hoped that the former might put some flesh on the generalisations of the latter.

As before, this work was undertaken by the generosity of the Judith E. Wilson Fund, which enables the English Faculty to bring working writers to Cambridge for a couple of terms as Visiting Fellows. To the late Judith E. Wilson, her friend Edith Evans, to her Trustees, and to the Faculty Board of English I am truly grateful.

While, sadly, the former Master of Trinity Hall had died, his successor Sir John Lyons, his wife Danielle, and the Fellows made me most welcome back in that college; it was a great pleasure to renew old friendships there, to enjoy their hospitality, and to make new friends there and elsewhere. I must also thank my old friends Alexander and Amira Goehr, Heather Glen and Gareth Stedman Jones for looking after me during this time.

Dr Peter Holland succeeded Raymond Williams in taking special responsibility for Drama in the English Faculty, as Judith E. Wilson Lecturer in Drama. As ever, he was a good friend, and I thank him for his practical help, and his enthusiasm.

I would like to thank Linda MacKenney for permission to quote at such length from her as yet unpublished book on *Popular Theatre in Scotland*. I must also acknowledge the quotations from Sir Roy Shaw's discussion document for the Arts Council of Great Britain; Professor Jan MacDonald's pamphlet on *A Citizen's Theatre*; Alisdair Cameron's letter to Chapman Magazine, and the anonymous authors of the publicity leaflet for the Gold Card Theatre scheme. I hope they will allow me to use their words to put a point of view I do not share.

I must thank Susie Brown for her hard work, care and help. My own family, Elizabeth MacLennan, Kate, Finn and Danny know how much I owe them, and how much they have sustained me, kept me going, during the times I am writing about.

I'd like to dedicate this book, for what it's worth, to The Resistance, to those who have had their lives distorted or destroyed so others could consume; to those who insist that co-operation rather than individual possessiveness is the better principle for the future happiness of humanity; may they survive, and that principle bring more joy to the lives of more people.

Edinburgh, December 1989

# Poisoning the Water

Mao Tse-Tung, in one of his cunning letters of advice to Party activists in China, said that the revolutionary must be like a fish, moving among the people as fish through the sea. A fine image, one which I used in 1973 in the title of a play written for Liverpool Everyman Theatre, *The Fish in the Sea*. At about this time the image was also noticed by the then Brigadier Frank Kitson, who, after triumphing over the Commies in Malaya, and the Cypriots in Kyrenia Castle, was in charge of counter-intelligence in the North of Ireland, once the Troubles broke out again in 1968/69. The good Brigadier observed the power of this image, and concluded that if this was the case, the job of the counter-insurrectionary forces was:

> To do something to the water which will force the fish into a position where it can be caught. Conceivably, it might be necessary to kill the fish by polluting the water. (*Low Intensity Operations: Subversion, Insurgency and Peacekeeping*, 1971)

The polluting of the water consisted of: a systematic management of the ways news and information of any

kind got out of Northern Ireland, and the rigorous
inflection of its content, language and presentation;
to present the opponent in as odious, despicable and
criminal a light as possible; the creation of spectacular
events of 'black propaganda' value, which an infamous
Dublin cinema bombing is now reliably believed to be;
the effective suppression of the point of view of the
opposition, including a total ban on radio and television;
the spreading of smears and innuendoes which are only
retracted after they have done their damage; and the
wooing of opinion-formers and leaders of the rebel
community with intimations of their importance to the
state and their future affranchisement.

During the ten years since the last series of talks I gave
here, the government of our country has, I think, and I
think we can demonstrate, used variants or imitations
of all the above techniques to poison the sea of Britain,
with the purpose of asphyxiating socialism.

As a theatre-maker who is not only socialist but also
committed to working with working class and oppositional audiences, and to presenting perspectives on our
society that do *not* point to the greater glory of the
capitalist system, I have suffered from this particular
pollution directly, and it has given me many problems in
my work. One such was the total withdrawal of funding
from it. And I would like to take the opportunity of
these talks to explore the set of experiences the last ten
years have brought. They are to do with quite specific
cultural, artistic, and theatrical questions, as well as
broader social and political issues; they are about the
notably different atmospheres of England, north and
south, and Scotland – lowland and highland, as well
as of other parts of the world; and sometimes touch on
problem-areas that I think are fairly central to how the

opposition to the corporate state can make any progress at all. They raise questions which are uncomfortable for the left as well as for the right, and some fundamental questions which must be answered before we can move on to new and better work in the 90s.

*        *        *

In 1979, in *A Good Night Out*, I described the work of 7:84 and other theatre companies in playing to working class and non-theatre-going audiences, and the experiences, cultural, personal, artistic, that had led me to turn away from a career in 'Mainstream' theatre and film and television, and spend my time writing, directing and organising shows to tour round the places where working people usually went for their entertainment, shows which had direct relevance to their lives, and the story of their class. One of the main planks of the work was the need for 'class-consciousness' in the working class, that is, knowledge of, solidarity with those with common interests and roles in society. Through the 60s and 70s this concept of 'class-consciousness' raised no problems: people knew what it meant, and knew it existed, and could chart its growth. Now, ten years later, the concept is unfamiliar, a word for something that no longer exists, something that failed.

Mrs Thatcher recently went so far as to question the idea that we live in a thing called a 'society'. 'What society?' she asked, with fearless intellectual rigour, 'we don't belong to society, we are all just individuals, doing the best we can for ourselves.' And what could be fairer than that? All these social structures no longer exist, they are irrelevant; like Marx's ultimate state, they have withered away. Far from being *class*-conscious, we are now not even conscious of being part of society as a whole! I presume the concept of patriotism transcends this argument, but otherwise she has no doubts that people should see themselves as belonging to groupings no larger than the family, and the only thing we have in common with others is the desire to do well for ourselves: this we have in common with everybody – some may have succeeded, indeed some spectacularly, others may have had less success – some none whatsoever – but we are all trying, that's what keeps us both together and apart.

This magisterial refutation of Marx, Weber, Lenin and the whole of sociological thought in the twentieth century would be laughable, if its purpose were not so plain, and its effects – as imposed on the self-perception of a great many citizens of the USA – so palpably beneficial to the forces of reaction.

Its purpose is to fragment, disperse to the winds, the remnants of class-conciousness in the British working class. Because it is from this root that there grew all the organisations of labour, the trades unions, the parties of the left, the political philosophy that has overthrown capitalism in many parts of the world, the political will to unite to improve the conditions and pay of workers in Britain, the desire for more social equality, better education, better health-care, better housing, better care of the old, the sick, the disadvantaged of all kinds, and consequently less take-home profit for the few. From this root of class-consciousness grew the possibility of those socially underneath combining, uniting their forces and resources, in order to overturn the social order. Dangerous stuff, revolutionary, inflammatory and leading to an atheistical communist dictatorship, as in Nicaragua. (Or in the Pentagon image of Nicaragua.)

The purpose of this idea that we are Not A Society is palpable.

So there was I, basing my whole artistic practice on the concept of 'class-consciousness', and there was the leader of my country telling me it didn't exist. What is more, she was going to make certain it didn't exist, by telling people, over and over again, very slowly, that it didn't exist. And this was only the first method of disintegrating the nation. There were many others. All of them played a major part in the way I was able to work.

The second, and most obvious method was the systematic destruction by a series of governments with large majorities, of all the *institutions* of the working class, the very embodiments of class-consciousness. The trades unions obviously had to go, or be refashioned in the image of American unions – providential societies, offering discount mail-order sales, pension- and private health-care schemes, old folks Christmas parties and holiday packages on the Costa Brava. So ASLEF was humbled, the teachers brought to heel, the AUEW under Gavin Laird turned into a toothless, compromised, strike-free zone, the Electricians under Hammond not even fit to stay in the TUC, and the doughty miners under Arthur 'the Horned Serpent' Scargill beaten into submission, physically smashed, sacrifically slaughtered by the media, and finally split in two, in a move that Frank Kitson must have savoured. With the unions smashed up, the TUC itself had little to sustain any militancy it might have had; it is now split, and largely ignored. It plays no central role in public life.

The Labour Party itself was subject to a succession of splits and natural disasters, not to mention a media black propaganda campaign that made the Dublin cinema

bombing look amateur. The creation of the SDP, so
earnestly supported by Norman Tebbitt, made sure
that the Tories would be able to keep on slipping
in between the SDP and Labour. If Labour had ever
embodied working-class consciousness, both were seen
to be humiliated throughout the 80s.

But the third reason for the disintegration of this very
consciousness was the Labour Party itself. In common
with almost every Social Democratic party in Europe,
and Australia and New Zealand, it has undergone a
dramatic, or some might think suspiciously well-co-
ordinated change in its purposes. The old Parliamentary
Labourism made endless compromises in a desire to
show it could make capitalism work better than the
Conservatives; the new-ish Crosland/Gaitskell revisionist
tendency, based on the quietist assumption that most
people really can't be bothered with politics and should
be allowed to dig their gardens, led to a fear of mobili-
sation of any kind. But now we have the new responses
of Labour to its crushing defeats in the 80s: the crock
of Gould at the end of the rainbow. In the 80s the
Labour Party had capitulated almost entirely to the smart
efficiencies of the market economy, which of course leads
them to an acceptance of an individualist, competitive
ethic. They justify this by their need to attract the
middle-class and professional-class vote. They end up
no longer the expression of the class-consciousness of
the working class, but as 'the party for all the people'. Of
course their emphases are different, and some policies,
including their arts policy, very conscious of the needs
of the working class, but their philosophy has shifted
crucially from collective to individual action, and motivation, and so from class- to individualised consciousness.

The fourth contributory factor is one that has long

been a feature of the British working-class – the 'self-improvement' ethos, which has now become an extreme reluctance in many if not most working-class people to call themselves 'working-class', indeed to regard being called that as something of an insult. Apart from the sturdy yeoman tradition of not wanting to be pigeon-holed, stereotyped or dismissed, this self-perception is also based on a sense of the possible inferiority implied by the phrase 'working-class', and a desire to assert that 'we' are as good as 'them'. Nevertheless these same people also have long held a great loyalty to the institutions of labour and to the local 'culture' of the working class – the pride in being Yorkshire, or Scouse, or Brummie; the pride in local dialect, traditions, places; the fanatical pride in the football team; the clannishness, exclusiveness, distrust of strangers; the love of local jokes, songs, comedians, pubs – all these still unite people in an ambivalent way: at times purely local, at others symbols of solidarity. A great many theatre companies around Britain drew on just this sensibility to draw in the crowds, and to present them with longer perspectives, wider horizons, unexpected connections.

Of course the working class has undergone a very significant change in the last ten years: unemployment has split it in two, creating a sub-class of very young and older people mostly, who no longer see the name 'working' class as meaning them. In some ways they see themselves as 'opposed' to and by those in work, who pay tax to keep them housed, clothed and fed. New, UB40 culture, is growing up with all the dangers of aimlessness and political instability traditionally associated with the 'lumpen' or 'ragged' proletariat.

Both extremes, of hysterical left and vicious right, use the frustration and energy of this sub-class to validate their own claims to represent the best interests of 'the people', undermining the desire of the 'working' class to be known as such, and splitting the identity of interest within families, streets, neighbourhoods. The drug culture, heroin abuse and prevalence of AIDS in some high-unemployment schemes unfortunately gives the unemployed a 'leper colony' reputation among many 'decent working folk'.

Sixth, there is the new ideology associated with Euro Communism of the *Marxism Today* variety: the 'identity of interests' of many minorities will together create a major force: how often have they been glibly lumped together – blacks, women, Asians, the disabled, the jobless, the gays and lesbians, even 'kids'. Often these groups have nothing in common *except* being a 'minority' – which of course 'women' are not.

This ideology – based on the revision that abolished the 'dictatorship of the proletariat' – is a serious, thought-through set of ideas, and has split the Communist Party in fragments: one part clinging to the idea that the working class will lead a socialist revolution and so create a classless society, the other apt to characterise the actually existing working class as sexist, racist, brute macho dim-wits who belong with Tory backwoodspersons, indeed can be demonstrated to be locked in a mutually dependent endless negotiation with the ruling class. Needless to say, this belief, now widespread, has further diminished the role of the working class, and its centrality to revolutionary struggle, and so has made class-consciousness secondary to gender – and racial struggles. And of course alliances between such groups have been seen to be very insecure and short-term.

The growth and urgency of ecological and environmental issues has served to unite concerned individuals of all classes in an apparently overriding struggle against the destruction of the earth's resources by advanced industrial processes. In some ways the anti-nuclear movement drew many of the same disparate forces together, with the same effect of making concern for the survival of the planet more important than the overthrow of the ruling class by concerted working-class action. The Soviet Union's record until very recently has been used to demonstrate that the former does not entirely depend on the latter.

The absence of any clear and obviously relevant development in Marxist or Socialist political, social or philosophical theory in the past decade has led to an air of staleness and repetition in the writings and exhortations of the left in general, and of Labour politicians and Trades Union leaders in particular. Having been put on the defensive by a series of massive defeats, the ideologists of the British working class have failed to respond with much more than rhetoric, clever devices, or a masochistic glorying in the outrageous triumphalism of the right.

This has been further compounded by the fact that when significant developments did emerge, as in Ken Livingstone's GLC and the other successes of municipal socialism in the Metropolitan Councils, the councils were immediately abolished by an all-powerful Tory government.

To this I need not add that the immense propaganda machine of the Tory party and government, financed with tax-payers' money as well as the cash from big business, and the associated onslaughts of the press, have not made the presentation of working-class perspectives to the public any easier. Indeed there is a case to argue that without this image-factory working full-blast against

it, the class-consciousness of the working class would
never have declined as sharply as it has. In Scotland, the
main newspapers are not in the pocket of the Tory party;
this could well be a crucial reason for the almost total
success of anti-Thatcher politics in Scotland, and the
relative strength of the Scottish TUC and the unions.

*      *      *

This, of course, brings me to my theme, which I
hope to expand with graphic detail and in full lurid
Technicolour over the next few weeks. It is in the context
of the decline in working-class consciousness I have just
outlined that I have been working for the last ten years.
I have been working as a writer and director in theatre,
film and television; as Artistic Director of two political
theatre companies; as Producer and Executive Producer
in films; I started and now run an independent company
making programmes for television; I have worked as
Chairperson of the Independent Programme Producers
Association in Scotland, and on its Council in London
through the negotiations for Access to ITV and BBC;
and I've been a fairly active member of ACTT, the film
and TV union, the Writers Guild, the Directors Guild,
the British Academy of Film and Television Arts, and
of Equity, the theatre union. I am not a member of
any political party, but am of the libertarian socialist
left, and have led a moderately active life in politics in
Scotland, particularly in cultural politics, or the politics
of culture. More importantly, during the last ten years
I have written at least fourteen full-length plays for the
stage, one opera libretto, seven television plays, one
documentary and two feature films, as well as directing
most of them and a few by other writers. It has been a

period of almost continuously frenzied activity, since I last delivered myself of a set of talks here in early 1979, published under the title *A Good Night Out*.

Those talks, as I said earlier, depended very much on the importance of working-class culture both in itself, as a necessary expression of a distinct set of experiences and values, and for the wider reasons of the centrality of the working class *as a class* to social change – effective, revolutionary overthrow of the capitalist system and of bourgeois dominance in all areas. If this was the central role of the working class, then it was crucial it should (a) have its cultural values redefined and (b) achieve greater self-confidence and skill in producing *its own* images of itself, its history, of society, and of individual human experience of all kinds, rather than images created by and for the bourgeoisie. This perspective made the state of working-class culture a site of struggle.

There are certain questions which present themselves about all this in today's very different atmosphere.

The first is whether there can be any such thing as working-class culture still in existence other than the commercial product of trivial 'entertainment'. If this is all there is to it, why bother at all? Why not throw in the sponge and concentrate on 'educating' the working class to receive their first Holy Communion of 'high' culture – making the values of the élite available to the many?

While the expression of working-class experience is in itself desirable, is it necessary? And if so, is it at all necessary to do anything about it – ? Surely market forces will produce whatever there may be of value in this area?

The crucial questions for Marxists are those connected with the revolutionary role of the proletariat – which itself has been a subject of great contention. To many of you it may well have a quaint and rather scholastic air, as in the great debate over how many revolutionaries can dance on the end of a pin – and indeed one could well be forgiven for asking, in late 80s Western Europe – 'Which revolution? What role? Which proletariat?' – as none of these are even remotely on the agenda. To suggest that the correct organisation of the coming revolution should be the primary concern of socialists in Britain today does display a certain vagueness about reality, and a criminal neglect of other, more pressing priorities.

Nevertheless, the fact remains that an Establishment controlling Britain does exist, made up of powerful men (and a very few women) in the financial, industrial, military, and multi-national sectors, which finds allies throughout our civil society. Clearly in political circles, but also in the legal, judicial, police, Special Branch network, in the educational establishment, among many top professional people of all kinds, among the large land-owners, and, crucially, in the Civil Service executive. This mighty and altogether unselfconscious set of people – just individuals doing well for themselves, as Thatcher would say – is ably and vigorously supported by the various American levers of pressure – NATO, the US Embassy, the CIA, and the World Bank – as well as the now very effective pressures from the altogether unelected officials of the Common Market.

This elaborate, many-headed complex is rather like the Gorgon, it cannot be looked at too directly: you will find yourself turned to stone. It needs to be seen through a mirror or a burnished shield. Unfortunately the owners of the shields and mirrors, Messrs Rupert Murdoch, Maxwell, Tiny Rowlands, even tinier Rees-Mogg, the owners of commercial TV stations and the BBC – i.e.

the controllers of the mass media – are not interested in playing Perseus.

So the beast lives on, grows ever more powerful, and – wondrous to relate – the more powerful it grows, the more invisible it becomes! Unlike other empires with their pomp and ceremony, parades of elephants, marching in triumph through Persepolis, the new Empire 'prioritises', as it would say, silence and stealth, discretion and low profile. It becomes very angry and vindictive when its low profile activities are made public, as when its Secret Service tried to undermine a democratically elected Prime Minister by a series of dirty tricks and smears. Some years later one of those Secret Servants revealed this humiliating fact to the world and They sent their most powerful Civil Servant into another country at the other end of the world to silence him. They failed. That is why we know about it. But in how many other cases have they succeeded? We don't know about them at all.

Silence and stealth, maintaining a discreet, orbiting surveillance of the world, and a low profile. Men not in gaudy uniforms but in grey suits, their orders not barked out by centurions but electronically-transmitted world-wide, rows and rows of even black print, persuasive, imperative. Our own native ruling class now more confident, their values more readily disseminated by their press, their TV, their teachers and academics, their operators on countless committees, boards, councils, corporations and trusts throughout the land. But never hysterical, shrill or emphatic: always calm, *douce* and understated to the edge of dullness.

We must try to remember these features of the new ruling class when we come to examine in later sessions the operations of the Arts establishment, the funding

authorities, the bland ranks of smiling Arts administrators.

It can scarcely be denied, given the spectacle of Tory
Party Conferences, that we do have a ruling class.
Interestingly, they are not at all ashamed of *their* class-
consciousness, they are almost exemplary in their class
loyalty, in their self-definition and projection, in their
internationalism and solidarity with their comrades in
difficulties – Pinochet in Chile, Somoza in Nicaragua,
the charmless rulers of El Salvador and Guatemala. But
at home, they are not often ostentatious, prefer to be
seen as family-men sharing homely problems with their
employees, nice to meet, sharp, intelligent and able to
afford to be kind and considerate.

If this then is the 'ruling' class, whom do they rule?
Or if we choose to see them as managerial rather than
proprietorial, whom do they manage? The preferred
answer is that they merely regulate their own small
area of other lives, including each other's, that they
have no community of interest, merely serve their own
imperatives in a small segment of the capitalist economy,
and so are not 'ruling' anybody.

But this won't do. We have seen their collectivity of
interest expressed in government activity for ten years;
we have seen their class-consciousness expressed in the
ideology of the radical right, now dominant. And we have
seen that while 'they' and those close to and supportive
of 'them' have flourished in the last ten years, others
have seriously declined, have suffered actual hardship
– physical, social and psychological – and that these
'others' do have certain common characteristics.

A great many 'others' exist whose whole lives are in
part – in certain vital parts – ruled or managed by the
ruling class; whose interests may not be identical, but

who have strong common interests; who may not have an adequate, shared ideology or set of assumptions, but who have opinions and priorities which oppose those of the ruling class to some extent, and which are constantly under attack; who may not be very articulate or sophisticated in a literary sense, but who have an experience of life which they need to express or participate in the expression of; who may not perceive themselves as of any particular class or group, who may certainly not experience their lives as 'oppressed' or see any other group as 'oppressors' – conscious or unconscious – but who when looked at objectively are not able to experience the same fulfilment in life that others clearly are: who are, objectively, oppressed.

This is not an analytical statement on class, nor is it definition by location within the processes of production in the classic Marxist manner. It is an attempt to identify the people in our society – who are I believe in the majority – who make up the opposition to the new dominant ethos, who are economically, or in other resources, net losers in the thrusting entrepreneurial society. For the time being I shall resist the impulse to define them further, to locate them either by their consciousness, or their roles in production, or their self-perception or indeed their income. I shall not define them as a class, nor give them a role in a revolution. I shall simply call them The Resistance, and note that they undoubtedly exist, and are almost certainly a majority of the population of the UK.

They are both the subject of and the audience for the kind of theatre, film and television which my colleagues and I are trying to make. It is their life-experience, needs, values and aspirations that I and my colleagues in 7:84 and many other companies have been working to articulate, using cultural specifics – language, entertainment values, comedy, music etc. – that are familiar to that audience.

⌐Clearly to some ideologues of the right, such work presents a challenge: a three-fold contestation. Firstly, it assumes there is a culture with a set of values other than the dominant ones which can be taken seriously; secondly, in that it gives a voice to oppositional forces, it is politically undesirable; and thirdly, in creating new forms, and content with a vigorous connection with lived experience which is normally disregarded, it challenges the attenuation and whimsicality of the new modes of the dominant culture.⌐ Consequently it has three main sets of detractors: those with a vested interest in culture as we know it – heads of arts organisations, most critics, art-lovers, theatre-goers, film-buffs and opera-fans; those with a vested interest in a right-wing political trajectory – the government, their place-men in the arts organisations, their supporters in the arts generally; and those who are dedicated followers of fashion, who write off such work as 'old hat', '60s', 'hippy' – therefore boring and cuttable.

Perhaps it would help to sketch in what we *were* doing, briefly.

After my term here in 1979 I went back to Scotland to find a country punched to a standstill by the double body-blows of the loss of the opportunity for devolution – brought about by a combination of weasel cunning and popular inertia; and the presence of a Tory government in Westminster ruling a non-Tory Scotland. In March 1979 a majority of those voting voted for the creation of a Scots Assembly. They did not get one. In May 1979 a small minority of Scots voting voted for a Tory government. Scotland has been ruled by one ever since. The writer Neal Ascherson described the atmosphere in Scotland as like the endless wait in the rain for an Edinburgh traffic-light to turn green. The set-up in 7:84 Scotland was such that we were able to decide to do something, there and then, that would give vent to the pent-up anger of many people at this double duplicity, this double denial of voice to the people of Scotland. It was not to be a callow 'protest' play, nor could it usefully be a naturalistic drama.

There was a great character called Joe Smith who lived in the Cowgate in Edinburgh in the eighteenth century, General Joe they called him, because if he heard of an injustice being done to a poor person, or if there was a cause to campaign for, he would wheeck on his drum, and beat it through the streets, until he assembled his army from the closes and wynds – three or four thousand of them, marching behind him to see justice restored, or a point forcibly made to the Provost and his Baillies. The conceit of the play we did then, called *Joe's Drum*, was to have Joe himself come drumming back from the grave, awoken by the thunderous apathy of the devolution vote, to berate the population today, and to trace the decline of direct action as he knew it, through the 'moral force' of the Chartists, to the occasional placing of a cross on a ballot paper.

*Joe's Drum* had all the elements of the kind of theatre we had evolved from popular entertainment forms in Scotland – a lot of songs, some new, some old; short scenes, mainly monologues to the audiences from a variety of characters; a lot of 'comic' turns, including one from Adam Ferguson, the Enlightenment philosopher, and one Nicholas Fairbum, an eccentric MP. We had also a longer scene based on the County Cork tradition of 'kitchen operas', relayed to us by an Irish member of the company, in which a story is told in song by the characters in it, with simple accompaniment and exaggerated mime. We used this to show a particular bread riot in Edinburgh. There was a song about James Connolly, who was from Edinburgh, though executed by the British army for his part in the Dublin Easter Rising of 1916, and Robert Burns's *Tree of Liberty*, or at least three sets of its many verses.

It was an outburst, a spontaneous cry of despair almost, a rallying-cry for the future, and a hard look at democracy in its changing fashions. It was conceived, written, rehearsed and on within two months. There was a long, six- or seven-week tour of all parts of Scotland, and large, happy audiences. There was trouble from those constituency Labour Parties who were against devolution – several were – and a small radical-feminist protest against the way Joe Smith treated his wife – and the fact that she wore a skirt. Apart from that, it went down well and strongly. I don't know if it could have achieved anything tangible – the damage had been done – but it made a lot of people feel more like fighting on, a bit restored. Joe was played by Bill Riddoch, a powerful actor who had been with us for six years by then; Joe Smith remains a figure in many memories in Scotland. We published the play, with the Aberdeen People's Press, and sold it for many years after.

That was all happening in Scotland. With the English 7:84 Company, we took a major decision on touring policy. Instead of trying to cover the whole country with every show – impossible – we chose the forty or so best audiences for the work. They were in halls, community centres and small theatres in Cumbria, the North-West including Merseyside and Deeside, Yorkshire, the East Midlands – Corby, Northampton and Nottingham, and even West End London. We decided to concentrate on building these audiences up by regular return visits, with at least two shows per year. By far the most popular and successful of these was a show about coal miners, called *One Big Blow*, by John Burrows, with an all-male, *a cappella* singing company (who later went on to become The Flying Pickets and to hit number one position in the Top Twenty, with a not very political song called *Only You*. In their wildly popular stage act, they still manage to combine ironic boyish horseplay with sharp, oppositional patter, as well as the odd song.)

Democracy came in for another, very different treatment in a piece I wrote to start us off on this circuit: *Nightclass*. Several members of the company were exercised by the use of words to deceive that had been, and is, the mark of Tory Public Relations – particularly words like 'freedom' – as in 'Freedom Association', 'free choice', 'freedom for enterprise', 'Free World', etc. They thought we should do a show based on this trickery. I responded with a show about Democracy – which aimed by its structure to uncover the hidden contradictions within that concept.

A young poly lecturer is about to do a course of extra-mural lectures on the British Constitution: he bursts in through the blackboard, an all-singing, all-dancing, even tap-dancing, medicine-man, come to sell his patent ideas. As he unfolds his notions in song and dance – de-mock-ra-see! made a wonderful Greek knees-up – slowly the material reality of the four people who have come to hear him comes to undermine the idealism of the concepts, and to reveal a level of tragedy, and farce, in the lives of the class. Fred Molina played the lecturer with verve, bottle and amazing speed. The class were mostly new recruits to 7:84 England. The show toured the new circuit, and won us regular bookings for the next few years.

Nothing is more wearying than listening to the plots of plays, unless it is the plots of novels, and I apologise for doing this to you. I am trying to give an indication of the kind of work, the kind of company, the kind of speed of response, the kind of audience that we were able to achieve in the early 1980s. We are talking about less than nine years ago, we are talking about the 80s, but already it seems prehistoric. A theatrical genre can now go out of fashion as quickly and completely as last year's PG Tips commercial. The speed and totality with which history is being re-written over the last ten years is truly alarming.

The process of killing off this area of work is almost complete. The announcement in 1988 of withdrawal of funding from Joint Stock and Foco Novo just about finished it off. Now the process of wiping out the memory of it and/or discrediting its achievements is under way.

The Poisoning of the Water demands that the sympathetic presentation of socialist ideas, particularly to working class audiences, should be stopped. Their images of 'socialism' must now be received from *The Sun*, *The Star*, *The Mail* and *The Express*. Popular theatre, all popular culture with socialist values must be first rooted out and then discredited.

During these talks I hope at least to discuss the major developments in this area of work, in this country and abroad – developments of form and audience, of content and geographical spread, from Inverness to the Inuit of northern British Columbia, from Zimbabwe to New Zealand. I will also try to give, through my personal experience, some idea of the way the opponents of this area of work have set about stifling it in Britain: a complex story that involves an account of most of the mechanisms of cultural hegemony available to the rulers of western societies. I shall try to extend the scope of the narrative to include similar work in film, television and video, and I shall try to put forward a series of positive proposals towards an arts policy and an artistic practice for the future of popular theatre in this country. Times are changing, and I would like to use this opportunity not only to look at what was an interesting beginning, but also to look forward to an alternative theatre of the 90s.

# 2

# Against The State

In the first of these talks I described the many recent pressures on the concept of 'class-consciousness', at least in the working class, and the attempts to discredit, revise, fragment, or physically smash both this consciousness and the many institutions of the working class which are the embodiment of this consciousness. This is being achieved: one, through the promotion and dominance of the bourgeois ideology of possessive individualism; two, through destruction of the unions, the TUC and the Labour Party; three, through the capitulation of labourism in the face of electoral defeats to a variant of this ideology; four, through a reluctance of people to see themselves as 'working class', i.e. inferior; five, by the effects of unemployment, which leaves large sectors feeling not a part of the 'working' class; sixth, through the revisionist ideology of the *Marxism Today* variety, which by abolishing the 'dictatorship of the proletariat' and embracing the 'rainbow coalition' notion, has rejected the centrality of the working class to social change, which the 'green' movement also does; and seventh, the absence of any theoretical development of any significance on the left, and the destruction of any successes, e.g. the GLC and the Metropolitan Boroughs' 'Municipal Socialism'. All these forces were completed by the activities of the press and other media, and by the extraordinary insistence of Mrs Thatcher that none of us are part of 'a society' – just individuals doing well for ourselves.

I also described the odd sensation of being a theatre-maker who, as outlined in my book, *A Good Night Out*, bases a practice of theatre on the actuality of working-class class-consciousness, only to find the leader of my country telling me it doesn't exist.

Today I would like to look quite briefly at the changes in the nature of, and the perception of, another central concept: the State. I am not well qualified to speak of it scientifically, so I must speak mostly through my own direct experience of it, which I shall restrict to the experience of the 7:84 England Theatre Company. First, a few observations.

In classical Leninist politics, the State is the embodiment of the power of the ruling class, and the means by which it controls the operation of the whole of society, and reproduces itself for the future. The capitalist state legitimates capitalism, from which flow all the other structures and superstructures of the state, religion, tolerance, the educational system, the legal and judicial systems, etc. In order to enforce the will of the interest it represents, the State is, in Marx's words, in the end 'a body of armed men'.

Through the twentieth century many Western Marxists have elaborated detailed theories of precisely how the capitalist state maintains its position of control – notably Antonio Gramsci in Italy, but several including Ralph Miliband in Britain. They have sought to show how the capitalist state has tried to conceal this 'body of armed men' by an elaborate system of social and mental controls which the individuals in the population at large interiorise as 'common sense' or 'traditional' or 'the way we do things'. This self-shaping allows the state, normally, to exhibit a great degree of tolerance towards an acceptable level of dissent. Gramsci may have been writing in a Fascist prison, but Miliband was a professor in an English university. These intricate mechanisms of social and mental control or imposition of acceptance were called by Gramsci the system of hegemony: the key method of self-legitimation of the Western capitalist state. When this system breaks down, the body of armed men have to be called in, and this is neither comfortable, popular, nor ultimately effective (as we saw in Franco's Spain, Greece under the Colonels or Salazar's Portugal).

The capitalist system needs to develop, and this calls for intellectual and academic freedom, without which Spain for example, was slipping into the Third World. Its recent great leaps forward in industrial output have come under 'socialist' freedoms and could not have come under Franco. So the state prefers to keep the armed men waiting in the wings. The appearance of 'consensus' is therefore of material value not only to the state but also to the ruling class within the state.

One obvious method of gaining consensus, the one our society prefers, is for the state to define itself as being in the interests of the whole people, not just of one dominant class. Of course it is clearly in the interests of everybody that there should be a state of some sort, and it is easy to conflate this need for order with the need for the state we have – though it is far from certain that this state-structure is the *best* state-structure for a great many people: notably those sections of society we loosely characterised last week as The Resistance – i.e. those who are net losers in the recent reorganisation of society and redistribution of wealth.

In Lenin's scenario, the all-powerful capitalist or imperialist state could only be overthrown and replaced by a state in a more general interest, by the conscious, united and violent activity of the proletariat. This indeed took place in the Soviet Union, and has done with variants on the nature of 'proletariat' in countries all over the world. Problems arose in abundance in all of them, but few would deny that the emphasis in proletarian states has, at least nominally, been on the well-being of the mass of people, not on that of the owners of wealth.

These new, socialist states have also had to call upon bodies of armed men, and because more wilfully created, have been more in evidence, more visible as states rather than wise old traditional 'ways of doing things', more self-conscious. Consequently even though the British capitalist state has just as large, permanent and powerful a set of mechanisms as the Soviet or the Cuban, it is possible for Mrs Thatcher and her ideologues to talk of 'reducing the power of the state over people's lives' and to equate the bureaucracy that goes with certain labourist welfare policies with 'state control'. Her attacks on the 'Welfare State' – really the welfare *legislation* of more than one party – must not, therefore, be confused with a weakening of the powers of the capitalist State as such. On the contrary, as we shall see, these powers over the last ten years have been reinforced and spread with a determination bordering on violence into areas normally left to the loose liberal operation of hegemony. The identification of the radical Right's political will with the operation of State mechanisms has interestingly *politicised* the question of the nature of the state in a way that has undermined the 'consensus' that the British state is above politics, and has seriously worried that personification of our State, HM the Queen.

In spite of the immense and increasingly visible power of the British capitalist state, whether in its military imposition of its will in the South Atlantic or removal of ancient constitutional safeguards, like *habeas corpus*, the right to trial by jury, the presumption of innocence unless proved guilty, etc., there has grown up within the opposition to Thatcherism a strange compulsion to ignore, by-pass or even to scorn the centrality of the question of state power. This of course allows the role of the proletariat in the classical Leninist confrontation with the forces of the State to be conveniently avoided. The 'rainbow coalition' is essentially a defensive assemblage of the powerless, acquiescing in their own inability to change anything.

This then is another element in the *background* to the events which I shall try to describe in my own experience as lived in the 'alternative' theatre in England in the 1980s.

*        *        *

As I said earlier, 7:84 England had, in 1979/80, made a conscious decision to concentrate its efforts on a group of 40 venues spread over England, to build regular audiences for our work in these clubs, halls, community centres and small theatres. I have described our first show, *Nightclass*, which combined an ironic song-and-dance exposition of the British Constitution, a low-budget Bagehot, with the disintegration of the 'class' under pressure from the realities of their lives. It had a cast of five, a piano-player, and an ingenious set, some witty choreography and a lot of *joie-de-vivre*, jokes and songs.

As it was quite difficult to get to see any of this work unless you lived in Corby or Cleator Moor or Birkenhead, perhaps, at the risk of being boring, I should give a little more idea of the kind of shows we did during this three-year period.

*One Big Blow* was a piece about a miners' brass band, whose lead cornet-player could no longer blow as his lungs had gone. The band recruits a young chancer, against many better judgements, and he learns how to take his part in the music from the old miner. The Coal Board was present, meeting in a gymnasium amongst other places, and somehow, although deliberately not set in one locality, the rich culture of the pits of Britain and the communities around them, was lovingly, but not uncritically brought to life. The six, all male, actors we put together acted, sang *a capella*, and played the furniture. John Burrows, who wrote it after extensive improvisation with students and other staff in the Rose Bruford Drama School, created a production in the round which worked well, and suited the kind of venues we were playing – indeed could not have been done in straight theatres. This show went on a second tour, then a third tour in Scotland, and occasional revivals ever since. Our audiences loved it, and wanted more.

They got our version of Claire Luckham's *Trafford Tanzi*, also in the round, now very well-known from West End productions, and performed all over the world. For those who don't know it, it takes the form of a wrestling-match, between a woman and her man. It is about sexual oppression. The form of course was perfect for our work, the writing sharp and funny, and Pam Brighton's production had the audiences on their feet yelling and booing and at times over-eager to participate.

Jim Sheridan, who had been very much involved with us in the 70s, then went to found the Project Theatre in Dublin, came back to write and direct a bizarre show based on Hasek's *Good Soldier Schweyk*, apparently in the First World War, but somehow in Ireland, as he cycles and circles away from and towards the trenches in France. The set was entirely on wheels, cycles of extraordinary complexity which pedalled on prisons, offices, tents, the Allied lines, etc. An irrepressible cast, largely of Irish actors, was assembled, and the velocipedes rolled. One of the leads, a 7:84 regular, broke his arm the day the Arts Council visited us – they managed to make it to Highgate – so the show was a bit under-pedalled that night. They gave it the sour plum look, and this show was subsequently cited as evidence of our artistic failure, but I still think it was wonderful, and so did the audiences. It was about Schweyk, or Spike as he became, it was against war, and for dogs, it was class-conscious and had an Irish dimension, but above all it was about the pleasure of the theatrical imagination, the giddy fantasy that theatre can at its best induce, and which is at the core of the true value of that experience.

The bikes cost a fortune, then rusted away. Jim went to run the Irish Arts Centre in New York, to write the biography of the Irish fly-weight, Barry McGuigan and to make films, back in Ireland.

Different indeed was Barrie Keeffe's short-ish play *Sus*, about a black man picked up by the police. It was naturalistic, brutal, foul-mouthed and shocking, and gave audiences something to worry about. It touched on working-class, and police, racism, and the institutionalised racism of Britain: a moving, powerful statement, a dramatisation of an area of great concern, and an eye-opener to many. We took it to black communities as well as our regular audiences, and shocked both, with its direct accusation of the police, and its virulent language.

Half of a double bill by Peter Cox called *V-signs* also worked in the area of black oppression, this time indirectly and more psychologically. The other half was the monologue of an unemployed white male worker in Speke, Liverpool – a very moving, strong account of what happens to a person who believes in the dignity of labour, when the indignity of unemployment is forced upon them. It found a lot of response in our audiences.

Finally *Rejoice!* which was my answer to *My Fair Lady*. A woman social-worker in Liverpool confronted with the need to raise business sponsorship for her Addicts' Centre goes with her friend to see a businessman at his home. They take with them a black youth who has attached himself to them. The businessman, a bit of a wag, bets them the money they need that if they leave the boy with him, he can turn him into a good Young Conservative in three weeks flat. With a resounding aria, *Believe In Yourself*, he begins the boy's education. Three weeks later it is complete. So complete that the boy rips off the businessman for a lot of money, and sets off into the yuppie world, with both the skills to succeed and a deep desire to destroy it.

In this collection of plays, we were expressing, without I hope being too schematic or mechanical, a series of responses to the major social crises in the working class following the onslaught of the Tory government of 1979. At the same time a number of other com-

panies in different ways were voicing their perceptions:
Gay Sweatshop, Monstrous Regiment, Women's Theatre
Company, Temba, Black Theatre Co-operative, Graeae,
as well as more general programmes from Foco Novo,
Joint Stock, Red Ladder, Belt and Braces, North-West
Spanner, etc., and the radicalised reps or studios, like
Liverpool Everyman, Liverpool Playhouse and Studio,
Sheffield Crucible, Manchester Contact, Nottingham
Playhouse and even occasionally the National Theatre
itself. A wide range of oppositional theatre was not
only permitted but was in the ascendant. True, the
Arts Council had cut its grants to 40 companies in
1980, including many on the left, but in the early 80s
Alternative Theatre of all kinds was making the running
in England. The best young writers, directors, designers,
actors, and technicians were working in this sector, and
the most interesting formal and material developments
were coming from it.

In the five years since 1983, this sector has been
effectively shut down in England. In exploring *how* this
was done, we may find out *why* it was done – and we
may encounter the reality of the capitalist state and the
changing modes of its hegemony.

I found a note I made in September 1978: 'Political
climate one of inertia; a kind of baffled exasperation
. . . The de-fusing policy of Callaghan *et al*, brilliant in
its self-denying thoroughness, has reduced all struggles
to trivial squabbles over methods. This, combined with
high unemployment levels, fear of more rejection from
the multi-nationals and even the nationalised industries,
and the cutbacks in government expenditure, has created
a feeling of retreat before uncomprehended forces . . .
(hence) a major source of reluctance to fight back: who
is there to fight?'

It is as well to remember that the 'swingeing cuts' were begun by Denis Healey in 1978, that the greatest disaster to the working class of this country since 1929 and Ramsay MacDonald's *volte face*, has been the Callaghan government, and that the pressures to put the state machine into a more aggressive mode in defence of capitalism were due to the economic crises experienced under a Labour government.

In my area, the distaste for 'community arts' and 'political theatre' were voiced most clearly in 1979 by a Labour appointment as Director-General of the Arts Council, Sir Roy Shaw. One of his first actions on taking office in 1976 was to reorganise the routine of the work of the Council in a way that marginalised the advice of the large panels or committees made up mostly of people working within the art-forms – and aggrandizing the Finance Department under Tony Field. In 1980, Roy Shaw cut 43 companies, and paved the way for Rees-Mogg.

In October 1982, Roy Shaw produced a discussion paper on Politics and the Arts Council for the Council to discuss, from which I'd like to quote a few passages:

A number of the theatre groups take up a political position well to the left of the Labour Party, whose social democratic reformism is held to have collapsed, of the trades unions and, indeed, of the Communist Party which is seen as having turned away from revolutionary politics. Hence, according to Itzin, 'the left and its theatre were faced with the lack of a clear Marxist alternative to the existing political parties, and with the constant question of how to relate the theatre to political reality'. John McGrath, founder of 7:84, the subsidised company operating both in Scotland and England, declared in 1970 that 'In this country the time is ripe for revolutionary socialism to make itself known as a real alternative to the failed "pragmatism" of the Labour leadership,' and urged the need 'to oppose bourgeois theatre by creating a truly revolutionary theatre in order to help bring about a change in society and in our own art'.

It is ironical that Brecht had similar beliefs, and yet his plays are now regularly performed by our two national theatre companies, supposedly the home of 'bourgeois theatre'. Is this because time has, as with Verdi, muted the political message, or because Brecht really embodies this message dramatically in a way which often eludes some of the latterday left-wing theatre groups? I have walked out of performances by the 7:84 Company and Belt and Braces simply because I objected to being given a political lecture instead of a dramatic experience. I stayed through 7:84's *Yobbo Nowt*, where a small audience of the converted frequently burst into applause, not for *coups de théâtre*, but for political utterances with which they agreed. The occasion was more like a political meeting than a theatre performance. (7:84 is currently touring a new play *Rejoice!* which the Director of the North West Arts Association says is loaded with political dogma.)

In *Stages In The Revolution*, Itzin profiles about a dozen socialist theatre groups, all grant-aided. If asked to justify giving them grants, drama officers and panels would say that the productions are judged solely on their artistic quality and not by political criteria. If the 'message' becomes too strident, in other words, if the purpose is mainly propagandist, then this will impair the artistic quality. So we would agree (with some qualifications) with one of Chairman Mao's better 'thoughts': 'Works of art which lack artistic quality have no force, no matter how progressive they are politically'.

Lack of artistic quality can, for example, manifest itself in presenting a picture of industry where the workers are all saints and the bosses are all wicked, foolish, or both. Reality is more muddled and subtle than that. An example of a play which presented such a simplistic view of life was Howard Brenton's *Weapons of Happiness*, performed at the National Theatre. To be fair, however, one should remember that many outstanding plays came from left-wing writers who emerged in the 70s; Trevor Griffiths' *Comedians* and David Edgar's dramatisation of *Nicholas Nickleby* are but two of many.

I have referred frequently in this paper to the declared political aim of artists. To decide whether these aims are achieved is beyond my scope, for it would require not only a detailed analysis of many works of art, but also sociological research to discover what the effects were. Much left-wing theatre, for example, simply preaches to the converted – and often to rather small audiences. (Anyone who disagrees with their views could argue, however, that to confirm, or 'harden', these views is undesirable.) Some playwrights themselves question whether they have any real effect, and it is certainly ironical that the decade when left-wing drama flourished as never before, ended with the election of Mrs Thatcher's government. Nevertheless, Professor Martin Esslin, a former Chairman of our Drama Panel, believes that a thorough study of political theatre in the past clearly shows that 'plays are not very useful as short-term tactical weapons in the political struggle; but they are immensely powerful in establishing long-term, decisive changes in consciousness – lasting political results'.

What may be more questionable is that artists expect public money to advocate the overthrow, not of the particular party in power, but of the whole system of parliamentary democracy.

Lord Goodman, when Chairman of the Arts Council, questioned whether it was the duty of the state actually to subsidise those who are working to overthrow it. This question remains. Some years ago a study of English theatre compared this situation to that in Max Frisch's *The Fire Raisers* in which a middle-class muddler goes on being polite and helpful to two arsonists who have designs on his house. It is a point that the Arts Council will have to consider carefully . . .'

The Arts Council of course did consider it. Very carefully. Its Finance Director, Mr Tony Field, he of the greater powers, gave a paper, called 'Experiment and Public Accountability', to the Second International Conference on Cultural Economics and Planning in Maastricht, Holland, with this as his main burden:

In the period from 1970 to 1980 the Arts Council experienced such a growth and gave priority to the development of drama groups. This is demonstrated in Appendix I where each year's additional commitments can be seen to develop a growing pattern. (The named companies are those which, in the course of time, became regular Arts Council clients; the remainder are contained each year under 'all others' which include the relatively few which received grants for projects and which never matured successfully enough to warrant subsidy for regular annual programmes of work.)

My contentions are that:

a) too many groups received regular annual subsidy to the extent that they became increasingly reliant upon the Art Council;

b) too few groups were given project money; in other words the Advisory Panel for Drama and the Council's officers (including myself as Finance Director) failed to build into the system any constructive flexibility;

c) the principles of assessment used during the period of growth were not sufficiently explained to and accepted by the profession so that they could be retained as a proper method of assessment in times of more restrictive funding;

d) the standards of assessment adopted for the Council's regular annually subsidised clients do not necessarily apply to groups formed to experiment.

Under (a) it was often the case that the subsidising

body genuinely considered it was exercising flexibility in, say, the case of Welfare State where the grant at the outset was a modest £1,124, then £8,820 and then only £13,000 and so on. However, the input of subsidy which, almost unwittingly became regular, persuaded the group to go on and on, often far beyond its really creative development. The extreme example of this is, perhaps, the English Stage Company which came into superb flowering under the brilliant George Devine. On his lamented death, the subsidies continued to the Board of Directors (six characters in search of a policy!) and the bricks and mortar. Better perhaps to have announced: 'Here is a theatre with subsidy for someone to run for three years and three years only'.

Mr Tony Field goes on to say that reps are different. But he too was laying the groundwork for Mogg. Both he and Roy Shaw were firmly of the Weskerite School, what Alan Sinfield of Sussex University calls 'Left Culturism', the belief in the workers ultimately being educated to 'High Art', which is of universal and eternal value, self-evidently transcending barriers of class, language and epoch. What Tony Field and Roy Shaw did not appreciate was that their efforts to appear ruthless and cost-effective were not going to be enough.

On 3 May 1982 Sir William Rees-Mogg took up his post as Chairman of the Arts Council. By August 1983 Roy Shaw had gone. Soon after, Field left. He went to the commercial theatre. Roy Shaw continues to campaign to 'defend the arts'.

Sir William, or Lord Mogg as he now is – for services to the state – has a fascinating pedigree. He was educated at an English public school, Charterhouse, where he was Head of School; Balliol College, Oxford, where he was President of the Oxford Union. He was then on the staff of the *Financial Times*, was City Editor of the

*Sunday Times*, and from 1967 to 1981 Editor of *The Times* itself. He is, or was, proprietor of Pickering and Chatto Ltd., antiquarian booksellers, was for some time a very influential Deputy Chairman of the BBC, and has been a Director of GEC, the General Electric Company, since 1981.

This immaculate interweaving of inherited privilege and the City, power over broadcasting (which he was not slow to exercise), and even greater power in the newspaper industry, along with the standard eccentricity – antiquarian books – makes Mogg a walking personification of the very mechanisms of hegemony in all their suavity that Gramsci and quite specifically Miliband's *The State in Capitalist Society* had described. He combines in himself the links between the ruling class, the financial establishment, the industrial powers, and the 'organic' intellectual. He was appointed by Thatcher, as 'one of ours'. She would not have needed to give very detailed instructions, if any at all – the bonding was complete. By August 1983 she had won her second election, and the 'hardening' of the State's involvement in all areas of public life, part of a political campaign to destroy the welfare legislation and socialism, was set to enter a new phase. I often wonder if Mrs Thatcher or her advisers have not studied Gramsci better than the left – indeed whether they have not appropriated Rudi Deutschke's 'Long March Through the Institutions'. She certainly set about consolidating the corporate nature of the capitalist state, re-affirming its basis as the legitimation of the power of capital and private enterprise, and incorporating every aspect of public life into its detailed control.

To complete the machinery, Roy Shaw was forced to resign by the swishings of the new broom, and the little-known but egregiously charming Luke Rittner was appointed in his place. With limited knowledge or experience of the arts, Rittner had one significant qualification: he was Director of the Association for Business Sponsorship of the Arts. Whereas Shaw had scowled at Rothmans getting the credit and publicity for 'sponsoring' an opera production that the Arts Council had paid for, clearly Luke had the new gospel under his arm, and would facilitate the entry of business money into the arts. There would be no trappings of Wilsonism here, no ideological baggage: he would do the jobs; he was the contractor.

A great many of the best of the staff left at this time, and were replaced with difficulty and without distinction. Within two years Tom Sutcliff was able to write in the *Guardian*: 'The Rees-Mogg regime is in a sorry state. Instead of acting as the arm's length fulcrum between the Treasury and the arts institutions, it has started to mouth only the government line . . Like Mrs Thatcher, Rees-Mogg is presiding over present decline while parroting about a better tomorrow which existing policies put permanently beyond reach'.

Within one year of his arrival, and seven months of Rittner's, they produced a definitive document: *The Glory of the Garden*. Let me give you the quotation from Rudyard Kipling that sets the tone:

Our England is a garden, and such gardens are not
     made
By singing: 'Oh, how beautiful!' and sitting in the
     shade
While better men than we go out and start their
     working lives
At grubbing weeds from gravel-pits with broken dinner-
     knives.

To return now to the personal level of this story, one weed grubbed up by the broken dinner-knives was 7:84 England. It was working on an annual grant of £92,500. This was to be removed within twelve months.

We launched an elaborate appeal, nationwide and worldwide, which produced an overwhelming response. We were given a brutally short time to present an appeal document to the Arts Council, but we did, and it was impressive. Our record was clearly one of very high standards in all areas, the response of the public was overwhelming, and the support from the trades unions, the Labour Party, theatres and community centres, was unequivocal. The appeal was dismissed.

Rees-Mogg, in an assiduously PR-managed press conference, declared that our cut was based on 'artistic criteria'. People complaining were told our 'standards' were not high enough. Few were in a position to argue with the 'experts'. All this was trotted out in the press and on television. This was not the case, as became clear when, a few months later, a somewhat different story emerged. When challenged on the 'standards' of 7:84, they then wrote: 'The Council would wish us to make it clear that there is much to commend artistically in the company's work . . . the withdrawal of subsidy was made on strategic grounds . . .'

Nevertheless the offer made by Merseyside Arts, Knowsley Council and St Helen's Council to provide us with a theatre and half of our subsidy, had to be turned down when the Arts Council refused them permission to use the funds now made available to them to help 7:84. The 'strategy' was notionally to encourage arts provision in the regions. In our case the 'strategy' meant something else: annihilation.

\*　　　\*　　　\*

During the year left to us, we produced two major shows; one was a revival, with some restructuring, of *Six Men of Dorset*, a play first commissioned by the TUC in 1934 to commemorate the centenary of the trial of the 'Tolpuddle Martyrs' – six men transported for activity in an early agricultural union; the second was Peter Cox's *The Garden of England*, a play about the Kent miners and their families during the miners' strike that was still taking place. The TUC, in the person of Norman Willis, had persuaded some of their constituent unions – notably the Transport and General Workers – to produce some £45,000 to make *Six Men* – a very large production – possible. It had a good production by Pam Brighton, an excellent cast, and a triumphal tour, starting with an audience of nine hundred Yorkshire miners in the Sheffield Crucible Theatre, and ending with a blazing, packed run in the Shaw Theatre in London. On the first night at the Shaw, as the audience stood singing 'Raise Your Banners High', you could be forgiven for thinking that this was a new, exciting company just starting off with a huge and confident and victorious following: Neil Kinnock and Norman Willis joining in, in fine voice. 7:84 England had a few months to go. The Shaw itself is now (1989) closing as a theatre. And what is happening to Neil Kinnock? What is happening to Norman Willis?

I'd like, if I may, to read you some of my thoughts on the situation written at that time:

> It is a fact that several miners who had not before been out on the picket-line, went out and picketed, after seeing 7:84 England's production of *Six Men Of Dorset*. It is a fact that every single review of this production so far

has expressed astonishment at Sir William Rees-Mogg's decision to cut this company on 'artistic' grounds, and his stubborn refusal of all efforts to save it. It is a fact that tens of thousands of Trades Unionists in Sheffield, Liverpool, Norwich, Ipswich, Newcastle, Dorset, and South Wales have seen their own history on the stage, perhaps for the first time, and have been moved by what they experienced not only to the flash of recognition, but also to the will to act – even to act politically. Whether a work of art is improved or damaged by a direct political purpose is, rightly, a matter for lively debate. But it is a matter for some alarm when the guardians of our culture appear to have made it almost impossible for a work of art with a particular political message to be made at all. Especially when those guardians have astonishingly little actual qualification for making artistic judgements of any kind apart from their adherence to the political élite that appointed them: an élite itself incapable of inspiring any work of art, with or without purpose.

That this is indeed what is happening in England will be disputed with all the deadly charm of Dry Tory PR, but that it is the case is now generally, wearily, recognised. Wearily, since the assault on civil liberties, the bending of the highest principles of the law, the cruelty of our government's social policy, have all been painfully charted by many wise and good people, only to be oiled out of sight with a velvety sigh and a coo of ministerial reassurance. If they can get away with the Belgrano, they can get away with the sinking of political theatre.

*        *        *

7:84 England are not the only victims, nor is Lord Mogg the only executioner, though he has perfected his swing. CAST, a socialist group sending out to clubs all over the country variety acts that offered something other than strip and racist comedy, had their small subvention removed. Others, like Red Ladder, were 'devolved' – thrown on the mercy of local authorities, who have minimal funds, reduced even further by the government's direct intervention – and even more political volatility and venom than the Arts Council.

\*　　　\*　　　\*

Socialists, you will recall, wish to reduce all nature's variety to drab uniformity: remember Mao's uniformed millions, Stalin's monolithic architecture, the little brown clones of Ho Chi Minh?

And Tories, in case you had forgotten, love individuality, enterprise, independence of spirit. Sadly, this is as untrue in the arts as in business.

And the conceptual framework of what is happening in the arts in Britain is altogether consistent with the ideological shift that the government is trying to impose on the country.

In the theatre, the concept of national and regional 'centres of excellence' is the instrument to express the Tory longing for something to look up to. It is also neat, conveniently fundable, and good for absorbing any stray dissent.

In these shrines, 'standards' can be defined, and celebrated, and paid for, preferably by sponsors wishing their product to be associated with such 'excellence'.

The independent theatre companies, apart from being bureaucratically inconvenient, apt to have messy books and to give away tickets to the unemployed, were also difficult to have vetted in advance by 'responsible' people.

These companies, however, attracted a tremendous amount of new talent, who created new and vibrantly different ways of doing things. Any perceptive bureaucrat who cared for the future of theatre would have encouraged such free, intrepid and seminal companies to grow and flourish.

In England, we have had no perceptive arts bureaucrats for many a year. Mr Tony Field, ex-Head of Finance at the Arts Council, actually wanted these companies to have the life-span of a butterfly, then rapidly die.

*The Guardian*, our supposedly liberal and fearless newspaper, has as its chief Arts reporter, one Nicholas de Jongh, who seemed, at that time, curiously sensitive to the needs and desires of the new upper crust of the Arts Council. In the first of a series of uncomfortably well-informed statements on Arts Council policy, he also demanded the strangling of lame ducks and the axing of dead wood, which is Arts Council Newspeak for politically motivated cuts. And he betrayed an amazing weariness with life. When asked to come to a press conference in the House of Commons, for example, called by Neil Kinnock and the head of our Trades Unions, to announce their major support for a new 7:84 show, at ten-thirty in the morning, it was, he told me, too early. He failed to come along, or even mention that it happened. So even the ideology of the supposedly radical press has been transformed successfully into an instrument of Tory propaganda. There's no help from that quarter any more.

The ideological legacy of Mr Field's generation of arts bureaucrats is 'centres of excellence' – the National Theatre and the RSC, and the new regional theatres for the car-owning middle-class élite. They busily buy up all the bright ideas and people of the independent companies, and put them through the mincer of their production-processes, sanitise their ideology, cover them in gooey lighting, and they emerge no longer vibrant, different, startling or unique, but conformist, tame and toothless. If politics is to be allowed, it is certain to be the unedifying spectacle of left-wing writers presenting a travesty of their past allegiancies, or tearing their breasts in histrionic impotence. The consequences of this shift are serious for theatrical culture in Britain.

To return to the consequences for 7:84 (England). In mid-1984, Ken Livingstone and the GLC offered to put up money for an idea for a show I had suggested based on a funfair. It was to tour Leeds, Manchester, Liverpool and Birmingham, then run in the Jubilee Gardens on the South Bank, all in a Big Top. Socialist theatre was going to come to town with *All the Fun of the Fair*. I shall return to this notion of Carnival as a positive way forward later, and indeed make it the main theme of my last talk here, when we come to being I hope, a whole lot more positive than I may have appeared so far. But there is still a deal more drama to unfold before then.

In Spring '85 our Arts Council subsidy was withdrawn. Our fully subsidised life came to an end. John Burrow's production of *Garden of England* opened shakily to 3,000 miners, families and suppporters in Sheffield Civic Hall: they willed it to work, and in the end it did. Newcastle, Liverpool, Manchester, South Wales, all in huge venues with not even standing room, turning away thousands. Here, in the audience, was what I called last week 'The Resistance'. A combination of trades unionists, working-class people, political activists, the women's movement, gays, many unemployed, old and young, they were delighted to be together, making contact with one another through support for the miners and for the event: a 7:84 visit. This was positive, a foundation to be built on. But we had been Mogged. It was not our first but our last visit – possibly ever.

And the next experience, in the year of the fall of the GLC, left some of us in despair not so much at the iniquities of the right, which were manifest, but at the insanities of the left, which were much harder to bear. In telling this story, I shall try to avoid a simple clash of personalities, and concentrate on what it tells us of the state of some sectors of the left in 1985, so that lessons may perhaps be learnt for the future.

My conception of *All the Fun of the Fair* was that it would be a travelling carnival of socialist politics and values. All around and inside the tent would be side-shows – Fortune Tellers, Aunt Sallies, Wheels of Fortune with loaded arrows, Try Your Strength machines, Hoop-tossing over objects just too large – all the hucksters operating in true Tory Spirit, taking your money, offering glittering prizes, but making it just impossible for the punter. The show itself was to be a series of scenes from modern life cast in the mould of or based on fun-fair or circus images – of Roller Coasters, the Wall of Death, Freak Shows, Punch and Judy – with a band and songs in between. I was excited by the prospect, bubbling over with ideas, eager to get it going. We were pricing Big Tops, finding sites and raising extra cash with GLC help from the other Metropolitan Boroughs in the North and Midlands - who were all keen to have us during the summer of '84.

I was advised, and agreed, that I would need a director, as writing and organising was quite enough. So I approached a good director – let's call him Rupert. Rupert had worked as an actor with 7:84, and had gone off to start his own company – to avoid 'the power of the pen' as he put it. His company had had great success, but had folded after moving into the West End, which made him personally a great deal of money.

I went to see Rupert who received me cautiously, told me he was an anarchist-Trotskyist, and somehow, I still don't know how, persuaded me by the end of the evening that I didn't really want to write The Funfair, he certainly wouldn't direct it, but what I *really* wanted to do was to commission him to write and direct a play to be set in the tent about life on an oil-rig.

There was indeed a way that the idea of telling the stories of why a group of men from all over Britain were forced out into the North Sea to survive could have been quite good. Rupert wanted to flood the tent with water, build the rig in the middle, and play all the non-rig scenes in the water. There would be dry ice of course, and arthritis to follow. It was to be called 'Brittania Rig'. Various other writers were to be called in to write scenes, and/or songs. I later, much later, discovered that it was also to be an exposé of how the inner workings of the Labour Party betrayed the masses, but more of that later.

My admin team in London, let's call them Bill and Dave, went to see Rupert, and came back pouring scorn on Funfairs and agog with the thrills to come on the rig. Rupert was a great salesman, and could have made even more money in cars. They plunged in, booking the tent, the transport, the crews, the sites, the actors, the musicians – the designer, who soon had the set under way in a yard in Bradford, and the composer. All absolutely great, but at this point we still had neither money nor written offer from the GLC. Nevertheless the hard-pressed officials in the GLC were sure, confident, certain, etc. that the first large cheque would be with us – 'very soon', 'next week'.

We went into rehearsal not only without any money, but also without a script. Rupert had been having a crisis of some kind, and was a bit behind. With a great show of charisma he united the large-ish cast behind the idea of creating the show in rehearsal, and soon they were all – or not quite all – in a state which must have been similar to that in Jonesville in Guyana before they took the poison, or in Münster in 1533, when the Anabaptists' faith in John of Leyden, also an ex-actor, led them to stand in starvation in the town square with their arms held out expecting on the third trump to be bodily assumed into everlasting glory.

Of course such a movement has to have an enemy. This turned out to be me, 7:84, and Neil Kinnock, in that order. Ken Livingstone soon joined us, as we shall see. By the Friday lunchtime of the first week, the cheque still had not arrived from the GLC. What had arrived was an injunction from the Conservative-run Westminster City Council forbidding the GLC to spend any money at all except that specifically listed in the base estimates, sums identified the year before. We were not so listed. Therefore we could not be paid, at least by any straightforward route.

It was a cheap manipulation of the minutiae of the law for patently political ends – Mr Justice McNeill in the High Court had distinguished himself among the senior judges of England by saying, in rejecting a similar attempt to abuse the law by Kensington and Chelsea Council:

> It is now clear that the issue is one for the political hustings and not for the court. It is a matter of real concern that the court, exercising the power of judicial review, is increasingly, and particularly in this case, used for political purposes superficially dressed up as points of law. The proper remedy in such matters is the ballot box and not the court. (*If Voting Changed Anything They'd Abolish It*, Ken Livingstone, 1987, p. 219)

Lord Denning frequently thought otherwise. It may have been cheap, and it was certainly dismissed several months later, but as far as we were concerned, it had worked. We could not pay the wages by 12 noon on Friday – the greatest crime in the theatre. With mutterings the company agreed to wait until the Monday. We held a Board Meeting over the week-end, and the Board instructed me that we could not continue to trade unless circumstances changed – i.e. a cheque arrived or a firm, dated promise was given. The GLC officials were still pretty confident they would find a way to release the money by the following Friday, but would put nothing on paper.

On the Monday morning I (Enemy Number One), on behalf of the 7:84 Board (Enemy Number Two) on which sat Neil Kinnock (Enemy Number Three), had to tell the company that Ken Livingstone (Enemy Number Four) had failed to deliver. We were confident that money would come by Friday, but we could no longer ask them to work for us, as we could not guarantee their wages, and would be trading while insolvent – making the directors personally liable for the whole deficit and liable also to go to prison. Needless to say I was deeply unhappy, and angry – and suggested our anger should not be directed at the GLC who were doing everything to help, but at Westminster Council and the Tory plotters and planners, who were desperate to discredit the popular and successful policies of the GLC.

The company invited me to a short Equity meeting, but as part of management I thought it inappropriate, and went back to the office. At this 'short Equity meeting' Rupert and 7:84's administrators Bill and Dave, told the bemused and angry company that the resolution to their problems was not to attack the Tories, not

to protest outside Westminster City Hall (this proposal
was defeated with the observation that if they tried that
they'd get their heads cracked open – a principled stand!)
but by a cunning plan. They would go the next morning
with blankets, and fruit and nuts into City Hall, the GLC
headquarters, and occupy Ken Livingstone's office!

There is not a great deal to be said about the personal courage involved in this fearless decision. Nor
about the political sagacity of handing the Tories a
victory on a plate – a source of merry propaganda
about the incompetent GLC, and a triumph in stifling
a Lefty theatre show. Nor about the likely practical
effectiveness in getting the show on by embarrassing
and betraying those who were already working flat out
to help us.

I learnt of this only after it had happened. I made
my way down the mahogany corridors of the GLC,
towards Ken's outer office, where they were – about
15 of them. I met one of the company on my way. Far
from the joy of battle I could see only a baleful terror
in his eyes, an aura combining nausea and puritanical
fanaticism in his face. 'Hi. How are things?' I asked
in a friendly fashion. The lips thinned, the pallor grew
paler. 'I'm not allowed to speak to you,' he said. 'If
you have any questions, you must address them to
the whole company, then go away. We will discuss
our answers and elect a spokesperson to convey them
to you, or not answer at all should we so decide.'
'Ah.' I said, flummoxed. He moved on in a soldierly
manner.

When I got to the office, Ken Livingstone's chief
aide took me off for a meeting with the Drama Officer,
an old friend from Scotland, and they told me of their
proposals, well under way before the 'occupation', to

present a cast-iron case at the Friday meeting which Ken Livingstone was to chair. They had a chance of lifting the injunction altogether by then, but failing that their legal people, with whom I also had meetings, were cautiously confident, as were the others involved. One of the problems they faced was that they had what amounted to two administrations in most departments, the new officers brought in, and of course the old bureaucrats left over, who had some seniority, and whose blocking power was legendary. I imagine a similar problem confronts Gorbachev in pushing on with *perestroika*.

Eventually the aide, let's call him Alfred, and I had a meeting, or put a set of questions to the owl-faced throng. Solemnly the spokesperson, given the go-ahead each time by a nod from Rupert, unfolded the replies. They regarded the GLC as morally responsible, and 7:84 as legally responsible, and Neil Kinnock as politically responsible – a point of view that has something going for it. They were to occupy until satisfaction of their demand; their demand was now not for money to do the show, but for money to pay their full twelve-week contract and *not to do* the show.

It was now impossible to do the show, they said, since as 7:84 had broken their contract they were free to find other work, and theoretically they might have. It was pointed out to them that the GLC would find it difficult to vote money to a show that they knew was not going to happen. They refused to reply to this. Little did I know then that Rupert, the writer-director-Svengali of the whole thing, had accepted another job already, to begin on the following Monday, acting in, of all things, a Ben Jonson comedy. This obviously made the whole thing utterly impossible anyway.

We spent the next few days up and down the mahogany, discovering a Byzantine world of intrigue and derring-do that had at its affable centre the smiling Ken Livingstone, undeterred by the horrific, ingenious, sometimes criminal attacks on him from the entire New Right and its media and 'black' propagandists.

The meeting on Friday voted us the money – cast iron, cheque on Monday. After the meeting it seems that the intrepid occupiers deliberately informed members of the Finance Department that they would not allow the show to go ahead. On hearing this, the Finance Director refused to issue the cheque.

The occupiers went off for other work or twelve weeks paid holiday. 7:84 was left with a commitment of £65,000, facing bankruptcy, unable even to pay its phone-bill.

The rest of the story is happier, in some ways. Ken and his people, with encouragement from our supporters, put together a package which enabled us to do a new show – *All the Fun of the Fair*, at last – and write off most of the deficit. Again there was drama over the cheque. It arrived in my hands with twenty minutes to go before the absolute deadline beyond which the show would be impossible. A race to the bank, and we were back in business. I had spent so much time in the corridors and offices that my concentration on writing the show was not what it should have been. Chris Bond directed at the Half Moon, and it suffered from its painful gestation: it should have been a thing of great joy: it became bitty and bitter. The critics, new and old, did not enjoy it – but I was happy that it pointed, in its style, to a way to the future.

Our troubled ally, the GLC, was abolished by Thatcher one week after we opened.

I shan't draw conclusions from all this: most are obvious. But I dare say Mogg was pleased. And Luke had done his job. Yet in the chaos and bitterness of *All the Fun of the Fair* lay the seeds of what I now see as the future, or a future.

# 3

# Popular, Populist, or Of The People

In the last talk I touched on the mechanisms of control exercised by the Western capitalist state, and described how, contrary to recent assertions, the power of the state is growing stronger, is penetrating ever more intimately into our lives. A practical example of the way this hegemony operates was given in the story of how 7:84 (England) was removed from active life, and how the activities of some people on the left gave support to the forces which now are putting state power to serve ever narrower political and class purposes.

This week I'd like to talk in a general way about the notion of cultural diversity, and the way centralised power combines with an ideology of 'excellence' to move towards a standardisation of cultural work. I'd like to examine briefly the ideas about 'national' culture, and in particular the Gramscian idea of the 'national popular', and to look at the opportunities for regional diversity within a European economic framework. In this context I would then like to look at some of the projects I was involved in with 7:84 (Scotland), to see how they fared against the onward march of the standard-bearers.

First, though, a brief explanation of my own personal 'cultural diversity'. A branch of my family did indeed settle in Kintail on the west coast of the Scottish highlands, and were spelt MacRae, or MacRha, but my McGraths did no such thing. They struggled on in Ireland until the end of the last century when they came to seek their fortune, or at least a living, in Birkenhead, over the Mersey from Liverpool. My mother's parents, the McCanns, came even later, and tried to be still spiritually in County Louth for the next two generations. Our community was the close-knit 'Liverpool Irish' network, rarely moving more than a few blocks from the dock wall, and the warm embrace of Our Lady's Church. One grandfather and three uncles were merchant sailors, and the other grandfather was a boilermaker in the yards.

To complicate the issue, when I was very young, my family was evacuated to a village in North Wales, and for various reasons stayed there until I was 16, so that my whole school life, as opposed to family life, was in the Welsh tradition. I was taught Welsh at school, my friends were the children of ex-coal-miners, steel-workers, small-holders, long-distance truck-drivers and railway workers. My teachers were emphatically Welsh, and my feeling for nature was inescapably Welsh. When we moved back to Merseyside I felt both a coming home and a terrible sense of loss. The density of the Liverpool culture of the time, made up strongly of its Irish and Welsh communities, spiced by the cosmopolitan additions of a great seaport, and moulded into its own highly verbal, scatological, witty and fantasy-prone style, was one that I rejoiced to re-embrace. And part of that Liverpool mixture is a sense of nostalgia for a rural past, shared by most of its members: I felt it more immediately, and strongly.

It was six or seven years later, after National Service in Germany, Egypt, Jordan, Malta and Libya, and after the ritual alienation of Oxford University, that I was taken by romance to a small village in the North Highlands, Rogart, in Sutherland. Here in the Highlands I discovered a living cultural identity that made instant contact with the traces of my Irishness and the feeling for nature – and much else – of my Welsh childhood. I came to live there for long periods, became involved in its struggles, present and past, tried to learn its old language and to understand the richness of its ways. In time I got to know something about Glasgow, Edinburgh, Aberdeen and Dundee, and now live most of the time in Edinburgh, for reasons of work, with long spells in the Highlands.

The purpose of this autobiographical rambling is not to present myself as the archetypal pan-Celt; it is to say that each one of these cultures of which I am privileged to be part has to me a totally distinct landscape, an emotional and linguistic and interpersonal specificity, a distinctness from every one of the others which is complete, yet with a variety of contiguities. Each one is a world in itself, each one in its different way a full and satisfying language for living together with, and for thinking, feeling and creating with. Each one is discrete, yet precious, containing values and priorities, ways of experiencing life, love, nature, human struggles, death and the spiritual which marks it out from the others, and makes its own contribution to the sum of human knowledge and the richness of human life.

Let us now turn to twentieth-century industrial methods of production, and the habits of mind and social organisation towards which they tend to lead. I shall try to avoid the 'mass-production' cliché, which often fails to be a useful analogy for human behaviour, and rarely has the standardising effect on those employed in it that it is meant to have. Usually the opposite, in my experience. Nevertheless the social and cultural consequences of cheap but uniform products, and of technological advances in cultural production and distribution must play a large part in our story.

But more important still is the apparent need of every national industrial complex for the protection and regulation of its activities and the expansion of its markets by the 'nation state'. This was particularly true of the so-called imperial powers, whose rivalry led to countless colonial conquests and two world wars. Our nation state, the United Kingdom of Great Britain and Northern Ireland, has been one of the most successful, but is now in decline as a world industrial power. Not many of its industries are, as the ICI ad claims, 'World Class'. Our nation is made up of several nations, with varying degrees of sovereignty: in a time of crisis, as in Northern Ireland, they can be run by direct rule from London. Wales was conquered by England, so all concessions to sovereignty are achieved by appealing to England's kindness, usually by burning cottages or blowing up television transmitters. Sometimes by hunger-strike. Scotland made a 'full, incorporating union' with England of its own free will, so they say, and retained vestiges of national distinctiveness – legal, educational and religious – but lost its parliament. Many of the provisions of the Act of Union are now ignored, and there is a move to have the whole thing renegotiated.

On a real level, however, the industrial, financial, land-owning and professional ruling groups of Scotland and Wales are tightly bonded with their partners in England, and increasingly their industries, banks, lands

and practices are owned by English- or US-based companies. In a recent TV programme on the 'Englishing of
Scotland', it was revealed that almost every single important Arts administration post in Scotland, including the
Arts Council posts, was held by an English person. The
ease with which the Arts administrators operate in the
world of the new business-oriented Arts funding and
executive groups is entirely consonant with the reduction
of Scotland to a branch economy. It is not surprising
therefore that the 'Scottishness' of Scottish culture will
be a quality as perceived by and sanitised for either a
comprador-style class within or an assessing group from
outside Scotland.

The other division within the UK is that of class
– however loosely we care to define it. The bankers,
fund-managers and unit-trust controllers of Edinburgh
New Town are distinct in every way, including culturally, from the unemployed teenager on heroin in the
shooting-galleries of Muirhouse and Pilton. This creates
a problem for the bankers etc., several of whom are very
artistic, chair the boards of opera and orchestra, gallery
and theatre. The problem is that when they speak of
'Scottish' culture they mean one thing, but in reality
there are two things – in fact many more than two,
since although their 'high' Scottish culture is 'national' in
being the same from Dumfries to Kirkwall, there are very
many locally distinct 'low' cultures – each one having an
element that could be called Scottish, but always having
a unique character – in the case of the Gaelic culture,
having its own language and an ancient tradition of
high and low within it. Similarly in Wales, in Northern
Ireland, and indeed in England, there exist high cultures
which are 'national', and which relate to one another in
the way of cosmopolitan bourgeois culture, and there are

several differing, sometimes violently differing, low, or working-class cultures.

I shall use the word 'popular' to describe these cultures, but I must sound a note of caution. There are some historians who have recently observed that historically the rich have often enjoyed the thrills of what is called 'popular' culture, which has led them to conclude that the word 'popular' therefore embraces the whole people, rich, poor and wino. I do not agree with this conclusion. Many working-class people enjoy opera, but this does not make Covent Garden a haven of popular culture. I use popular to distinguish these cultures from the dominant high culture which the middle and upper-classes are mainly qualified to consume – through education, wealth and social conditioning – and which is aimed primarily at them. Popular cultures are similarly those of the mass of the working people in their areas, and are primarily made for and enjoyed by them. Popular culture, as I have argued at length, is the site of a long, on-going struggle.

This struggle is between various active strands of popular culture. Let us take, for example, the role of animals in the world. There is undoubtedly a strong element within both industrial and agricultural workers which is indifferent to the suffering and death of animals: bear-baiting of old, dog- and cock-fighting today, and the plebeian equivalents of upper-class brutality, hunting and shooting. When we come to animal circuses, the cruelty is not obvious, may not exist, but never really worries this element. On the other hand, there is now a sick sentimentalisation of animals, kittens with bows on, puppies with toilet paper, monkeys selling tea – with all the cuteness, anthropocentrism and distance from reality of Walt Disney, who plays a formative part in this element. There is a third element, which sees 'dumb' animals as receptacles for kindness, as chums, as man's best friends, which is excited by digging holes in the ice for whales to escape – a more benign form of anthropomorphism. There is a fourth element, a more astringent, more 'realistic' set of images, which is concerned with conservation of species of animals, with their general well-being, but is content to let them get on with being animals. Now all four of these attitudes to animals co-exist within current popular culture, and have their cultural consequences, form part of the web of values that make up a culture.

Of those four elements, a 'progressive' attitude would find the first brutal, brutalising and to be opposed; the second trivial, trivialising, and to be combatted in a different way; the third sentimental but not so harmful as the first two; and the fourth possibly the most healthy and in touch with reality. These value-judgements would inform a 'progressive' struggle for popular culture, and would affect attitudes to circus, Walt Disney movies, other animal movies and presentations on television, and the use of animals, animal imagery and implicit attitudes to animals in new work created for a popular audience. The struggle would be firstly to arrive at and articulate a 'progressive' position, and secondly to present it as a more attractive, life-enhancing and forward-looking position than the other three. This involves a positive engagement within popular culture, and a broad political, social and moral perspective which may or may not be within a particular culture.

Now there is a cluster of problems connected with this last statement which I'd like to tease out, before going on. Firstly, there is a school of thought which assumes that popular culture is totally unconsciously created, that the values of the masses are deep, mysterious, unpredictable things that no educated person dare meddle in, that they have some unknowable, irrational motive force, like the tides, or fate. Many academics think this way, maybe from a false sense of modesty, many middle-class writers do so from a deeper base of fear and ignorance. Yet these values are created by conscious, articulate, educated, politically-aware men and women: the authors of *The Sun, The Daily Mirror, The Mail, Woman's Own, True Stories*, the Oxbridge makers of television programmes and videos, the shrewd producers of movies, the highly sophisticated, super-conscious advertising and PR people; and of course, in the greatest medium of all, the law of the land, values are enshrined by legislators of some intelligence. The educational system may feel opposed to popular culture, but in fact contributes to it. There is, it is true, a groundswell of wisdom and belief which none of those agencies can penetrate very deeply, but which is in reality only the accumulation of human reactions to a particular world, filtered by received opinions. It is, I think, more from reticence or ignorance that engagement of serious artists and thinkers with popular culture is seen as either inappropriate or impossible. (By 'engagement' I don't mean use of popular culture as subject-matter, but as a medium to communicate with working-class people.)

The second problem is of a different order. It comes from those who are opposed to such an intervention because they oppose progressive politics. These people see that the forces that shape popular culture are on their, reactionary, side, they see that these forces appeal to the backward element in people (for example, in popular support for hanging, or blowing up Argentinians), they see that money is to be made from exploiting the sentimental, the trite element, as in calendars, whether with kittens, thatched cottages or sex-object images of women on them. So, because of their political or commercial or even religious investment in the status quo, they try to present it as 'natural', as the way people like it, as the wisdom of the people. They also pretend that any intervention, save their own highly conscious one, is suspect outsider interference, and to be mocked as naive social engineering with Stalinist motivation.

The real problem is much more complex. It involves both the character of modern industrial society, and the nature and control of the mass media.

The main developments in the last 45 years of industrial society have led to increasing separation of people in their homes, in family groups, during their leisure time. If not in their homes, in their family motor cars or on package holidays. The occasions for social exchange are much fewer. Even in the pub, the new saloon designs try to separate people into small groups; people don't speak much on the buses or on trains; shopping is no longer a social event, or affords very little personal contact in the average Asda. The old communities are increasingly broken up, new towns, commuter towns, dormitory towns, reproductive villages, housing schemes, inner city development, high-rise non-solutions – the signs of a mobile population of small, isolated groups. As the pace of close-down of the traditional industries increases, more and more people have to get on their bikes and go where the work is, leaving the old working-class areas to the bulldozer or the yuppie, depending on their charm, and their distance from London.

In these circumstances, the old social sinews of the culture are cut, and the new ways of life do not encourage either the recreation of the old or the rise of new cultures,

or at least, only the rise of very attenuated ones. The
pub, the football match, the shopping centre, waiting
for the children outside school, maybe a youth club
– where else do people even meet, let alone develop
a rich, unique and life-enhancing culture, in the new
conurbations of Britain? Often people don't even have
a dialect in common – though school kids usually see
that one is manufactured, being the one group with real
contact with one another and a real need for identity.
But school kids become young marrieds, and slope off to
breed in bungaloid cosiness. Not all are so soft-centred,
but there is a certain norm.

In the closeness of much of a communally-created,
shared, participated-in culture, what do these millions
of small, isolated groups receive? They receive the artefacts of the media: as listed before, press, TV, ads,
but including the law, religion, education and political
argument.

Now we need to return to the effects of mass-production
on the standardization of popular culture. The rule is that
the more units you produce, the cheaper the unit-cost
(and so the greater the profit). In press and TV terms,
this means the bigger the audience viewing, or reading, the
greater the income from advertising, and the more money
there is to spend on the programme or the article. The BBC
has similar constraints, and even though there are regional
'opt-out' hours (not many, with not a lot of money spent
on them), the BBC still pumps out the same culture from
the Scillies to the Shetlands – and now, with simultaneous
Cable Relay, from the Alps to Connemara. (When the
BBC buys a programme, it insists on having the right
to allow its re-transmission, as it is being broadcast in
the UK, over almost the whole of Western Europe).
The ITV companies 'network', i.e. share, nearly all

programmes, and pay for them proportionately according to their potential advertising revenue. The government's proposed de-regulation of broadcasting is designed to increase these profits by removing all socially-desirable restraints on this process.

So the implication is that live, communally-generated and experienced popular culture rooted in the traditions of long-established communities is on the decline, and being replaced by the consumption in small groups of a standardised, non-local, non-specific culture created by those very groups of people who wish to exploit the backward elements in popular culture for their own commercial or political ends, the people who oppose any struggle for popular culture as interfering with nature.

In what, then, lies the possibility of struggle against it?

In the first place, and this can't be said too often, it lies in the contradictions within the system. At one level, there are many millions of 'consumers' who are not content with the nourishment this provides. They resist it, either passively by receiving it and not feeling happy about it, or actively by going off and looking for or indeed making the kind of social communion that can draw on the old traditions of popular culture and/or create new ones. The pub, the club, sport, the amateur operatics or drama group, political activity, union activity, the local church groups, debating societies, even the much derided folk-club have brought people out in quest of something. Whether they find it or not is another matter.

On another level there are many working in the supply of the artefacts who are not happy with their role. They do not wish to be seen as filling the gaps between commercials with the most appealing pulp, or, if they work for the BBC, trying to compete in much the same line, in order to hold a larger audience-share than ITV.

There are many in the religion industry who refuse to see themselves as dispensing opium to the people. Certainly many educationalists cannot reconcile what they have learnt with a society of possessive individualism and spectacular consumption at one end, and the deprivations of the Arrowe Park estate on the Wirral at the other.

Now this refusal or desire to do something culturally more valuable, classically leads to two main kinds of reaction. The first is to acknowledge the etiolation of popular culture among the people of many industrial areas, and to try to replace it with a form of High Culture, traditionally the preserve of the educated middle classes. Many great and worthy people have dedicated their lives to educating the workers and the uninitiated into 'appreciating' art, literature, music, opera, drama, the greatest in the world, from other times and other places maybe, but with something to say to, or to delight people of all kinds today. And I am the first to applaud their work, and to hope that it will be allowed to flourish. Sir Roy Shaw, last Secretary General of the Arts Council, considers this to be the main task of the Council today, and I have often told him that I and people working in my field are not opposed to this work. For propaganda reasons he and others like him choose to pretend that what they call 'community' artists are Huns and Visigoths, demanding the destruction of all 'high' culture from Langland to Henze, but this is not so. There are auras of exclusivity and hierarchy which we find distasteful, but that's just a matter of consideration for others and good manners, in the end.

So we get opera for free on Channel 4, BBC radio, BBC2, and opera very heavily subsidised in most of the Regional Centres. We have of course opera records, tapes and videos, operatic societies, and WEA classes in music appreciation in Harlow, Stevenage, Billericay and Cumbernauld. The Welsh are said, by Tony Field, to discuss opera in the pubs with more vehemence than they discuss rugby. Opera 'outreach' teams do missionary work in schools, the Scottish TUC sponsors the opening night of an opera in Glasgow and the unions sell the tickets. Opera-go-round takes studio productions to ever remoter village halls, and the audiences turn out for it. Excellent. The same is true to a greater or lesser extent of classical music, bourgeois theatre, literature and art.

Surely this is what is needed?

There is another response possible, the one which I and many others have been associated with, which is to see 'popular culture' as the site of an ongoing struggle. The reasons for this are many. One is clearly that the struggle for the 'progressive' within popular culture is close to the political struggle for working-class class-consciousness, for the empowering of the dispossessed, for the articulation and strengthening of The Resistance. I can't see how it can not be. The momentary successes of possessive individualist politics have led to a form of populist crypto-fascism in parts of the English working class that are terrible to behold. Politically, I think the care for a healthy, self-confident and progressive popular culture is of the first importance. From it flows all hope for the future.

Another reason is to do with a concern for that diversity of cultures which is so valuable to humanity as a whole. And here we come to look again at the idea of 'the nation'. As a construct for ruling people, utilised later for protecting capital's interests, the nation has, as we saw, a strong relationship with high culture. But on the level of popular culture it had no great meaning until the arrival of television, a mere thirty years ago. Geordie culture was quite distinct from Cornish, Manchester even more from Liverpool, East End from Sheffield. In Scotland, as I said, one of the popular cultures even had its own language, and for all they understand each other, so might Orcadians and Glaswegians. Girls from the Highlands still feel 'foreign' in Edinburgh, lads from Leeds would be 'uncomfortable' in Hampshire. Many people see a need to work to keep alive, to give confidence to, those many languages of distinct cultures, not to preserve but to develop them as the regions change, as new forces come in. Leeds becoming an amazing centre for dance, with mostly black dancers, is not a break in, but a development of that culture, and local people are proud of it.

It has to be said that both the 'education' to high culture and the commercial pressures of the media are winning: they are standardising British popular culture in a way that Germany has experienced. Now local traditions are of antiquarian value only and are marketed. Local differences are vestigial and like the fields of East Anglia, their boundaries, hedges and coppices are being smoothed out under the plough.

I do not want to preserve a set of cultures for the sake of the museum or their antiquarian value as commodities. The effort to work in a local popular culture is only worthwhile if it is alive and means something to the people of the area. But making that effort is what many of us consider of the greatest importance.

\*　　　\*　　　\*

Having said all that, I'd like to turn to some of the ways we set about this kind of work in Scotland, with the Scottish 7:84. It is in the context not only of popular cultural struggle but also that of the operations of the

*Scot finance)*

capitalist state, and that of class-consciousness that I'd like to set this account. I'll only talk of the five years from 1979 to 1984, and the work in Scotland.

In the first session I talked a little about going back to Scotland after being at Cambridge for a term and writing *A Good Night Out*. The first play was the blast against apathy called *Joe's Drum*, in 1979. One of the more bizarre after-effects of my eight weeks in Cambridge was that everyone remotely connected with the Arts Council came up and said in a particular tone of voice: 'Ah, how nice to see you – tell me, when are you back from Cambridge?' This went on for three years. Only a month ago I met a Glasgow accountant, then a member of the Arts Council. When I told him of my recent difficulties he said: 'Ah yes, but you were always away in Cambridge.' When I asked him how long he thought I had deserted my post, he backed off and generously conceded it may not have been for much more than a year. This was odd, but symptomatic. They wanted me to be away, and there was something they sneakily sniggered at about me as a 'man of the people' selling out for the fleshpots of the Cam. But there was also an air of peevishness about the tone of their question, and a definite sense that this had been the subject of some superior speculation.

Anyway, I was here for eight weeks, went back in April 1979 and *Joe's Drum* was on in September. After this necessary outburst, I began to talk to people about strategy, to think about a way to cope with the Thatcherite 80s. We made various quite different approaches to this problem. One was to soft-pedal on the agitational politics and to expose more gently the realities of the way class works in our class society. One was to chart the epic story of a fighting woman, from pugilistic girlhood through family struggles to leading a successful strike to being thrown out of work and betrayed: an attempt to recapitulate how we got to Thatcher. A third was a hugely ambitious project to re-write the history of twentieth-century theatre in Scotland by a season of neglected plays from working-class theatre, along with talks, readings, concerts etc., to make a major impact in Glasgow. The fourth was to go back to the Highlands with a new show about what was then going on in and around the Minch. The fifth was an attempt to branch out into a bigger series of great plays from the popular theatre of the past, and of other countries. The sixth was involvement in a new festival of popular theatre and music for Glasgow, called Mayfest. The seventh was the making of a new popular theatre base, teaching centre, workshop and rehearsal space in the middle of Edinburgh. These were not separate stabs at the problem, but are connected with a wider strategy of asserting the strengths of Scottish popular culture, now and historically, of broadening the perception of popular theatre by pointing out it had a history and world-wide spread, and of laying some foundations for the future.

To take these approaches one by one. In *Swings and Roundabouts* I wrote a play actually conceived as a variant on Nöel Coward's *Private Lives*. But the two couples in the adjoining bedrooms were separated by class, not age or divorce as in Coward's play. In this play I offered no authorial comment, no 7:84 explicit political line, no songs with messages. It was set not on the Riviera but outside Falkirk in a concrete hotel called the Neptune's Fork with a view of the oil refinery at Grangemouth, and a multi-tartan-panelled dining room and lounge. A working-class bloke, incapacitated from any marital activity by wedding Pomagne superimposed on hangover from the stag party, collapses on the bed leaving socially-ambitious secretary and new wife with nowhere to go. In the next room a furious executive has had to seek refuge because his car broke down with him and his new wife on their way to a honeymoon on Skye. She is what is usually called 'hopeless', an upper-class woman who creates a neurotic chaos around her. She has managed to start her period as they left for the honeymoon, and is not really sure she wanted to be on the honeymoon anyway. With some jiggery-pokery on the adjoining concrete balconies while watching the burn-off flame at the refinery, frustrated executive and frustrated secretary go off to *rendez-vous* in the bushes. Hungover bloke and 'hopeless female' meet, and talk. Nothing sexual happens to any of them, but on the way a lot of the minutiae of the class war are brought out. At one point the young worker is humiliated by the executive. Rosemary, the upper-class woman, goes off into a rhapsody. It's about working men like him. I think it might be relevant to read a bit of what she says:

> The whole of North America used to be carpeted with roving herds of buffalo. Sixty or 70 million faintly ridiculous creatures, looking like a cross between a camel and a Highland cow, but they were immensely strong, and very useful – in fact they provided everything that human beings needed to live on – food, clothing, even wigwams were made from buffaloes. And when they moved together in a stampede, nothing could stop them; they used to turn over railway trains, and chop the pioneers in their covered wagons into little pieces as they thundered by in their thousands, for hour after hour. But on their own, each one was too kind – and too trusting. A skilled hunter would creep up on a herd, then pick off the leader. The others would look to see whether the leader was worried, but no, he would just stand for

a minute or two. So the others would graze on. Then he would topple over; those very near would perhaps take fright. And then some others would come up to look at the dead ones, and sniff them, and they would throw up their heads and bawl. So he would shoot them. Then usually a bunch would run off, but he would shoot their leader, and the others would turn back in dismay and swirl around, and the idea was that the hunter could keep them milling around in circles for as long as he liked, just shooting those who tried to start a movement away from the centre. (Pause.) In this way, one man could kill one hundred buffaloes in an hour or two. In 13 years they killed about 40 million, till there were only a hundred or so left on all the rolling prairies between Texas and Calgary. (Pause.) Poor buffaloes. They ended up as leather armchairs. Or glue. (Pause.) What will you end up as, Andy?

*Swings and Roundabouts* had an interesting tour. It was remembered by many of the less political people who came to see it at The Citizens Theatre, Glasgow, as one of our most effective pieces. In the Gents at Paisley Trades Council they reckoned we'd gone soft, were backsliding. It was maybe the sort of play that needed to be done in England more than in Scotland, but still an important thing to do, and horribly prescient. It was written in December 1979 and January 1980. This is a little of Freddie, the Executive's thoughts after his weekend:

It's been fashionable for some time to pretend that class doesn't exist any more in Britain. The proles trying to disguise themselves as respectable bank managers, the youth inventing this 'class-less' get-up, with woolly sweaters and Dacri-Nylon trousers and party-frocks. The socialists claiming that they were the party for all, and Ted Heath burbling on about the 'Property-owning democracy'. Yuk. Well, that's all gone, thank goodness. What this country needs is a strong and a rich, and a

confident layer of men, to run it efficiently. Motivated,
dedicated chaps, who feel in their water that their ideas
are good, and are right, and will work. If those men
don't appear soon, and assert their authority, and seize
the possibilities of the new technology – Britain is doomed
to joining the Third World in 20, no, ten years' time.
Those are the facts; and at last we've got people running
the show now who aren't afraid: of the facts, or of the
consequences. They're giving motivation, and incentive,
to management: but more important, they're giving them
the confidence to be what they are: bosses. Upper class.
Leaders of men. And if this country is not to degenerate
into some sort of Ethiopia, the gap between those men in
the upper classs and the proles who carry on their orders
must get bigger; and it is getting bigger. (*Angrily.*) Where
are those bloody people? I don't say this as a political
argument – not at all: this isn't politics. It's survival.
I know. I'm a management consultant, I study the
workings of industry: top, middle and bottom layers. I
know what's wrong. I see it every day. The confidence of
management has been undermined. The placidity of the
workforce has been destroyed by notions of democracy
and equality. Well industry isn't democratic, and they
are not equal. (*Angry.*) Waiter! As far as I'm concerned,
this sort of place is perfect for them – this is their prize
for voting Labour. Fine. They can have it. The spoils of
victory. We can sell them this over and over again, here,
in Blackpool, on the Costa Brava – and they are happy
with it. Look at that wee man – a satisfied customer.
Good. The new working class are happy with their new
baubles. Excellent. Now just let them stop whining for
more, and let us get on with running the country, or
we're all in for trouble. You might think I'm a snob. Or
a power-maniac. I'm not. You could say my problem is:
given the situation that we're in, and the system we live
by – I can see the solutions. I get very little pleasure
out of all this. Most of my life I'm fairly miserable. I
can't have – straightforward relationships with women

any more: my first wife just couldn't stand my . . . demands. Rosemary – hm . . . I just don't know. She's very – compliant. No, my life's not a bed of roses. Don't go thinking I'm a happy man. But at least I don't have to stay here any longer. (*He looks at his watch.*) Must go in search of a receptionist. And then, on – to the mysteries of the Corrie Vrechan Hotel, Portree; with whatever consolations lie in wait for me there.

The next show, still in 1980, was *Blood Red Roses*. Again we were trying to engage the audiences of the industrial areas in their own history, in analysing how we got to where we then were – in August 1980. The form of *Swings and Roundabouts* – an inversion of boulevard comedy, was not in our main tradition as a company. With *Blood Red Roses* we were telling a saga, and we used short scenes linked by a sung ballad, announced with a scene title, date, and place, and nature of government. It was a big story with a small, but strong, cast, including Liz MacLennan, Phyllis Logan, Bill Riddoch, a clever, apparently simple set by Jenny Tiramani, and ballads set to traditional melodies. It was very popular in the industrial areas, and we had to tour it again the following year. It played for three weeks in Edinburgh during the Festival, then toured to Whitfield Labour Club, St Andrews, Dundee, Glasgow, Clydebank Town Hall, Ratho, Arbroath, Erskine New Town, Shotts, East Kilbride and Livingstone New Town, Cumbernauld, Musselburgh, Aberdeen and memorably – the Scottish TUC Women's Conference in Stirling Miners' Welfare. It was a story very close to their experience, and was received line by line with vigorous response.

Two things were notable about the rest of the life of this show. One was that I was later able to make a three-part mini-series for television from it. The other was that we took it for a couple of weeks, as an experiment, round our Highland audiences – Tain, Brora, Wick, Thurso, Rogart, Ullapool, Stornoway, Tarbert Harris, Kyleakin on Skye and Inverness. In the more industrial areas, Thurso, Stornoway, it went down a treat. In the quieter, rural areas there was some disappointment: this is not one for us, they told me – and they had different attitudes to industrial battles, and to the abrasive character of Bessie, the heroine. There was, in plain words, a clash of cultures. They had come to expect from our Highland shows since *The Cheviot* not only a show directly *about* their lives and their history, but also in a form that related to their own kinds of entertainment.

I discussed the question of form very closely with friends from Rogart, and they were quite clear that a show that drew on the ceilidh form, that used Highland music, characters and comedy, that spoke their language in other words, meant far more to them than 'Southern' shows, no matter how theatrically excellent. This I had always believed, but it was interesting to have it confirmed so explicitly. My friends, I should say, were not of the local or incomer middle classes, but were crofters – men and women, road-workers, small shopkeepers and fencers. They liked our Highland shows because they were delighted to see their experience on the stage in their language. The 'white settlers' were the target audience for Opera-Go-Round, happier to tune in to Vienna. Which is not to say that our friends stayed away: they simply regarded opera as something else, a curiosity.

As a consequence of this, our next show, after we organised a brief but glorious tour of the English 7:84's *One Big Blow* round the mining areas, was a new

Highland Show called *The Catch*, or *Red Herrings in the Minch*. It begins in Blackpool, at the funfair where everybody has fun. But soon a young Scots woman married to a Manchester working man, and feeling sadly nostalgic for home, drags him off on a coach trip to Skye. When the coach stops beside a sea-loch in the evening, she hears the seals calling her, and won't get back on the bus. He, furious, rescues their luggage, but, as in the story of the Seal-wife, her coat is left behind. All this, you will understand, is far from naturalistic, and as they make their way across and around the waters of the Minch, the stretch between the Western Seaboard, Skye in the South, and the Outer Isles to the West, they discover that this seal-haunted paradise is in fact packed with military installations, plutonium-bearing vessels, torpedo ranges, low-flying Buccaneers, its waters are regulated by European Commission regulations that have killed off the small local herring-boats leaving it to the high-tech monster-boats from the East and Holland, and that NATO is building an advance airbase prepared for global nuclear war in Stornoway's sleepy airport. Here Chuck the GI appears through the wall and explains to them the strategy of blocking off the Faroese gap. They go back to get her coat in Blackpool.

This time the Highland audiences had no problem. We kept a log of audience comment and reaction for that tour, and it revealed an enthusiasm and sense of owning this kind of theatre, and a feeling of detailed involvement in what happened to it, that showed that our feelings for the form, our political identification with and public articulation of popular concerns and our on-going relationships with the communities were all receiving strong endorsement from large popular audiences.

*The Catch* was also critically well received, and played to 99 per cent in the Edinburgh Festival in 1981. Our next Lowland tour with *Screw the Bobbin*, drew large audiences to the name 7:84, but sent them away disappointed. Without any disrespect to any one of them, it was not a success because it was entrusted to a team of writers, director and cast who were basically interested in bourgeois theatre – in which they have all ended up, with considerable success – and not so much in popular theatre, which demands very different values and disciplines. It was the story of the Paisley weavers and it did not do a lot of good to the company with audiences or critics. It reminded us painfully that what we were doing was *not* a genre of high culture, but something else entirely.

That 'something else' was being pushed out of history and permanently devalued by the mainstream culture executives.

Our next venture was to try to combat this class bias, and to celebrate for modern audiences the achievements of some of our predecessors in Scottish popular theatre. That is maybe a good point to begin again next week.

I'd like to end by going back to where we began, to the question of the value of a diversity of popular cultures to humanity as a whole. There can be no doubt that such diversity now exists, my own experience proves it beyond any reasonable doubt. Equally there is no question that there is now a strong, almost overwhelming pressure to weaken traditional cultures, rural or industrial, and to replace them either with standardised media product or with so-called 'universal' high culture. There are two main questions I think: one is the obvious – is it worth fighting for this diversity? And the second is – if so, what are the most effective means? Allied to this is the question of the whole class and political dimension of this struggle: is a thriving, rich local popular culture not as valuable a part of the environment at least as traffic regulations – and should local authorities and national government not be spending as much time, energy and money on it, as they do on traffic?

# 4

# Who Needs The SAS?

I have called this piece 'Who Needs The SAS?' which may be taken as a reference to recent events in Gibraltar, but really refers to the kind of abuse a socialist writer can expect, even from allies, even in Scotland. I'd like to read you a piece written recently by a fellow writer, whom I had taken for a friend; he writes of Scottish cinema as a 'quisling' cinema:

> The term 'quisling' may be unfamiliar and possibly even meaningless to film-makers who are under 30 and afflicted by the kind of mental myopia that is the ironical side effect of too much preoccupation with images. So some explanation is probably necessary . . . My dictionary defines quisling as 'a traitor who aids an occupying enemy force, a collaborator'. To those tempted to dismiss my accusation as an alarmist and politically unilateral outburst, I would like to make it quite clear that my condemnation applies equally to those who articulate loudly, perhaps too loudly, their devotion to the trendy left. My experience shows that such people are essentially safe middle-class people no different from the social worker who Peter Laurie stigmatises as 'soft police'. I will believe in John McGrath when I hear that an SAS hit team has arrived in Edinburgh with a hit list

that contains his name. As things are, he presents absolutely no threat to anyone, except perhaps to audiences who are susceptible to death by boredom.

In the same week that that tribute appeared, it was revealed in *The Observer* that I was high on the list of 'dangerous to employ' people circulated by the Economic League to employers in England. A week later I was refused a visa to attend a film festival where a film of mine was showing in Czechoslovakia. I say this not to claim the St Sebastian Award for strategic penetration, but to show that there is another side to nationalism, and a vicious side to the left.

In this talk I'm afraid I shall have to be very personal and detailed in order to be quite specific about the malaise of the 80s. I hope you will forgive this. It is far from being self-indulgent, I can assure you. Last week, we began to look at concepts of cultural diversity; we saw that a bourgeois 'nation' may produce one 'national' culture which is coherent, but also harbours several more local or regional 'popular' cultures. In this context we began to look at the work of 7:84 (Scotland), and saw that what meant a great deal in the Western Isles may not mean the same at all in Fife, and that Highlanders may not feel so excited by the problems of an industrial militant as Clydesiders; and we looked at the way the very language, sometimes the whole language, as in Gaelic, sometimes the complex historically-formed cultural language of the people, can be very different. And we looked at the way the forces of industrial society are tending to destroy traditional cultures, and replace them either with a lower version of high culture, or a standardised, commercial version of populist entertainment.

I broke off really in the middle of my account of how in

Scotland we began to try to tackle some of the problems these historical conjunctures set up for theatre-makers with our philosophy. I spoke about *Joe's Drum, Swings and Roundabouts, Blood Red Roses* and *The Catch*. I'd like to continue to look at the variety of what we have attempted, before coming back to the question of the possible future of 'popular' culture in a Tory, an EEC, and a Socialist world. On the way, I shall have to look at the ways the climate of the 1980s affected, and tried to kill, our work.

First, can I turn to one of our most interesting events – Clydebuilt. Linda MacKenney, who was at Cambridge when I was last here, came to help me research Scottish twentieth century 'popular' theatre, and really dug out most of the plays for the season. She wrote:

> John McGrath and other members of the 7:84 Theatre Company became increasingly aware of the tradition of working-class theatre in Scotland whilst touring 7:84's own productions during the last ten years. At the end of a show many people in the audience recalled other kinds of working-class theatre they had seen in Scotland in the past. People spoke to the company about Joe Corrie and his touring company of miner-actors, about Glasgow Unity, and the visits of Theatre Workshop, Ewan MacColl's plays.
>
> These discussions prompted 7:84 to research working-class theatre in Glasgow in the first half of the twentieth century. A search began for people who had formerly been involved as directors, performers, designers and technicians.
>
> Information about many theatre companies came to light and the actual scripts of a host of working-class plays emerged from attics and cardboard boxes under the stairs which revealed a rich strand of largely ignored popular theatre. Research continued with a view to reviving some of these original plays in new productions.

The four plays 7:84 have chosen to present may be seen as part of a 'tradition', a cultural movement which is, in turn, part of the history of the Scottish working class. They represent a kind of theatre which was made out of the history and experience of the working class, to be enjoyed in the first instance by working people – although, of course, they will be enjoyed by people from all walks of life.

I gave our reasons for this project rather more pretentiously:

Much of what is called the 'working-class struggle' is, in the long run, a struggle against the oppression or exploitation of the whole of humanity. While it may appear, quite frequently, that class struggle sets one group of human beings bitterly, indeed destructively, against another group of human beings, its ultimate purpose is to unite all people on a different basis: one of co-operation and unity in the common cause of defeating war, disease, hunger, lack of decent housing, ignorance and natural disasters wherever in the world they may be.

But this struggle is conducted in many different ways, some good, others evil. In the capitalist countries, the crimes of the left are never forgotten. Stalin's purges and murders and betrayals; the Kremlin's (and Castro's) treatment of dissidents; the brutalities of the Chinese Cultural Revolution; Hungary 1956, Czechoslovakia 1968, Afghanistan, Poland – where next? All these events are given maximum publicity by our media. They are used to discredit socialism, and to support a ruling class in Britain and America which has created the misery of unemployment on a massive scale in order to maximise profits, and has led humanity to the brink of an unthinkable war in order to prove that it is humane.

While the crimes of the left are trumpeted by the media, and many other, more noble acts are energetically represented as equally criminal, the victories and achievements of socialism are rapidly written out of

history altogether. Worse still, they are forgotten by the
succeeding generations working for the same cause.

In a very small way, this season of plays is an attempt
to remind our audiences both of the ultimate humanity
of the working-class struggle, and of the long, rich and
neglected tradition of the way it has been fought.

In Scotland, the labour movement has always had a
strong cultural side: it has generated its own poetry,
novels, songs, films and, of course, plays. But how many
of these works are in print, let alone read? I have no desire
to denigrate James Bridie, but it should be a cause for concern that he is *the* Scottish playwright of the 40s and 50s
– by virtue of playing to largely middle-class audiences.
The works of Joe Corrie, and the Unity plays, are 'not
remembered'. That means that they *are* remembered,
but by the 'wrong' people. It is partly in order to bring
to mind the cultural breadth and maturity of the Scottish
labour movement, that we present this Season.

From the naturalism of Joe Corrie to the musical-poetical
narrative ballad of Ewan MacColl, the season presents
proof also that popular theatre has a wide range of styles
and form, to take it way beyond social realism. Perhaps
the most exciting play in the season is Ena Lamont
Stewart's *Men Should Weep*, where many of today's
concerns with the position of women in society are shown
to have been debated in the working-class movement for
many years. Out of this has come a strong, vivid play
of Glasgow life, reminiscent of O'Casey and O'Neill.

In the course of the season we hope also to show how
theatre makes the connections between local divisive
class-struggle, and the common cause of the movement
towards a better life for all humanity – not just a few.
If they achieve that, they will have done their job.

In fact the season has to some extent changed the
map of Scottish theatre history. *Men Should Weep* –
interestingly the only play written by a middle-class
person – is now on many teaching syllabuses, and in

great demand still; Joe Corrie's work has become much
better known, and respected; Ewan McColl's part in
popular theatre-making is finally being recognised; and
the 'Unity' plays are now revived regularly in Scotland,
not only by 7:84 – though 7:84 has added *The Gorbals
Story* to the list, and put on a new play from Ena Lamont
Stewart.

The effects of the season were widespread. David
MacLennan told me that he and Feri Lean decided
that if we could do that, then they could start an
annual festival of popular theatre in Glasgow. In 1978
I had proposed a very similar festival to the STUC,
who had been enthusiastic, but it had not yet come off.
Our season was backed by Glasgow District Council and
Strathclyde Regional Council, as well as the Arts Council.
Glasgow District, the STUC and the Arts Council were
encouraged to put money into David and Feri's idea,
and it became Mayfest, which began in 1983 with a
company from Cuba; Pupi e Fresedde, a Commedia
dell' Arte Company from Italy; Gisella May from the
Berliner Ensemble; a host of British popular theatre
companies – many no longer with us, as they say –
who took the festival to the housing schemes and the
streets, and a new Scottish play in the Citizen's Theatre.
We shall come back to Mayfest, but there is no doubt
that it was part of that upsurge of Glasgow's pride in its
working-class cultural heritage that Clydebuilt played a
part in, and which is leading to the great hubris of
the 1990 European City of Culture title bestowed on
Glasgow by the EEC. That too we shall return to.

Clydebuilt aimed, amongst other things, to present the
plays in a variety of ways. We were lucky to find David
Scase free: he had acted the part of Johnny Noble in
Joan Littlewood's production of the play of that name,

and was then the director of the Manchester Library Theatre. He agreed to come and reproduce, as literally as possible, Joan's production. Johnny became a Scottish fisherman, but the wonderfully physical, free-moving, almost balletic staging inside a black box of a stage gave a great sense of its original impact, and the singing of the ballads by Dick Gaughan and a large cast was a joy.

With *Johnny Noble*, we put on *UAB Scotland*, a short piece of agit-prop from the Glasgow Workers' Theatre Group; it was vividly done, and done with great conviction, but this double-bill was the least approved of by the audiences – maybe because it was 'of its period', maybe because it was least 'Scottish'.

Of the two Unity plays, *Gold In His Boots* was a novelty, a play about football, but local politics, corruption, inflamed religious passions, romance, even murder all played their part. It was liked, and worked, but was odd – ultimately more interesting than satisfying. It was *Men Should Weep* that was the undoubted hit of the season. Raphael Samuel says he hated it, because it was not a working-class play, and it's true that Ena Lamont Stewart who wrote it was a 'daughter of the manse' – but it was certainly the play most working-class Glaswegians – and Londoners – identified with most passionately. The story of Maggie – played by Liz MacLennan – trying to bring up a large family in a crumbling Glasgow tenement, has the ring of a very deep truth to it, maybe speaking more to women than men. Giles Havergal did a completely modern, stylish production, that we brought back for the Edinburgh Festival, a tour of Scotland, and a visit to Joan Littlewood's old theatre at Stratford East. It was invited to Wyndham's, but we didn't go for various reasons. It is now regularly performed in Scotland and elsewhere.

I talked a lot to Ena, who is still going strong, and she told me a terrible story, which made me feel proud to have helped her at last gain some recognition. I asked why she hadn't written many more plays. She said she had, after *Men Should Weep*, written a play about the Highland Clearances. With great excitement I asked if I could read it. Well no, she said. She had sent it to James Bridie at the Citizen's Theatre, and gone to see him about it. He had told her to stick to comedy, and not write serious stuff. She was so upset, she went home and tore up the manuscript and burnt it. She hadn't written a full-length play since.

Bridie represents the power of the middle-class, middle-brow, complacent Scottish cultural establishment that has played, and is playing such a philistine, destructive, nevertheless self-congratulatory part in Scotland's history since Walter Scott played PR man to the Hanoverians. It was Bridie who caused the SAC Drama Committee to refuse to fund Unity and so to refuse to help it survive as a professional theatre. It may help to throw light on the realities of this cultural struggle if I tell you two stories from Linda MacKenney's book – as yet unpublished – on *Scots Popular Theatre*: first, James Bridie – who is still known as the greatest Scots playwright of the twentieth century – and his role in the demise of Unity Theatre:

James Bridie's conduct at the time of the Scottish Committee's withdrawal of Unity's guarantee was particularly suspect, for he was not only opposed to Scottish participation in the First Edinburgh Festival, he was also Chairman of the Citizen's Theatre Company, Unity's greatest rival. He had already shown himself able and willing to compromise his integrity for the Citizen's sake for – as James Barke first pointed out – he had used his authority as Chairman of the Scottish Committee to safeguard the Citizen's application for state funding. At the time of the Scottish Committee's decision to withdraw Unity's guarantee, Bridie was no longer Chairman. Nonetheless, his influence as a past Chairman and as an on-going committee member must have been very strong. Moreover, he must have been aware of the advantages that the Citizen's would accrue as a result of the removal of Unity from the Scottish theatrical scene. James Barke, who had a great deal of respect for Bridie's abilities – describing him as a 'dramatist of distinction' – was in little doubt about the immorality of his behaviour. He wrote, 'I think the time has come when Mr Bridie must face squarely the ethical consideration involved here.' Robert Mitchell, who likewise respected Bridie's abilities and his contribution to Scottish theatre, was deeply disappointed by Bridie's lack of integrity. Some years later, he reflected:

> It was a bad thing for James Bridie to have come to tell us our guarantee had been withdrawn. He was our rival in Glasgow at that time . . . and here he was – the Chairman of the Citizen's Theatre – being part of a deputation coming to tell another theatre they've lost their Arts Council support. I thought it was bad judgement on Bridie's part . . .

Unity was able to go ahead and take part in the First Edinburgh Festival as planned. When Robert Mitchell heard that the Scottish Committee of the Arts Council of Great Britain had withdrawn its guarantee, he was quite downcast and went to drown his sorrows in the Press Club in Glasgow. While he was there he got talking to James Swann, a Glasgow butcher, who had had literary aspirations of his own in his youth. Swann, with quite untoward generosity, offered Mitchell as much money as he needed and eventually subsidised Unity's visit to the Edinburgh Festival to the tune of £670.10s.0d. As a result Unity was able to take their Scots adaptation of

Maxim Gorki's *The Lower Depths* and Robert McLellan's *The Laird O' Torwatletie* to the Edinburgh Festival. Here, by raising a second furore in the press, by flouting the Edinburgh Festival Society and the Scottish Committee of the Arts Council of Great Britain's attempts to prevent their participation, they secured the maximum publicity possible.

They must have been very pleased with reviews, like that of Miron Grindea in *The Tribune*, who wrote that the most 'significant theatrical event' of the Festival was that 'sponsored by the Glasgow Unity Theatre'. He described the company in glowing terms: 'This was the only ensemble to provide a typically Scottish and technically perfect show . . .' He lamented the fact that it had been 'officially ignored' and drew his readers' attention to the irony of the situation, writing that although the company was 'considered by some people in authority as below international standards', it was 'greeted by critics and public alike as the best group of players at the Festival'.

Unity may have felt itself the victor in each of its confrontations with the Scottish theatrical establishment, but was in reality the loser. It could not have been otherwise. We may be sure – from the actions of the Athenaeum Theatre, the Edinburgh Festival Society and the Scottish Committee of the Arts Council of Great Britain – that the Scottish theatrical establishment was, at best, totally indifferent to Unity's need for or right to special support and, at worst, actively opposed to Unity's very existence.

Oscar Lewenstein was clearly seething with rage when he wrote the following:

> The Arts Council in Scotland, dominated by Bri-die and other reactionary elements, disassociated Glasgow Unity prior to last year's Festival on the grounds of 'low standards'. These grounds may be dismissed. The immediate cause was our insistence on Scottish representation at the Festival and the

basic cause a mixture of political prejudice and a fear
of the whole challenge to their cultural standards that
the work of our theatre is beginning to represent.

So far, so interesting.

Here's another of Linda's accounts, this time about
James Bridie and Joe Corrie – whose play *In Time O'
Strife* we revived for this season, in a naturalistic mode,
then again in a completely new, more 'expressionist'
production during the miners' strike. In case anyone
should be tempted to think that the neglect of this great
play was a mere accident, or had nothing to do with
class, let me read you another chunk of Linda's book:

Joe Corrie and the Fife Miner Players' relationship with
the music-hall and variety theatre seems to have had its
advantages and disadvantages. It proved an excellent
vehicle in Scotland in that it allowed the company to
reach a working-class audience beyond their native Fife.
However, they were unable to repeat their successes in
England and the fact that their plays and acting skills were
confined to the Scottish music-hall circuit meant that they
received little support from legitimate drama circles in
Scotland itself. Joe Corrie's play – as we have already
seen – made use of music-hall forms and techniques,
often with a view to attracting working-class people,
who traditionally attended music-hall entertainments.
Nonetheless, *In Time O' Strife* remained a piece of
legitimate drama and deserved to be recognised as such.
The fact that the play was presented in music-hall
theatres meant that its qualities as a piece of drama
were neglected by the drama critics attached to the more
reputable 'quality' newspapers (such as *The Scotsman*)
and by the members of other, *bona fide* Scottish drama
groups, notably the Scottish National Players.

During the 1920s, indigenous drama was still in its
infancy in Scotland. There were only a few drama groups
which specialised in producing Scottish plays and most of

these were amateur organisations. The Scottish National Players was one such group. It was formed in 1921 by Glaswegian middle-class people. Their aim was to found a 'Scottish National Theatre' which would match the successes of the Irish Players at the Abbey Theatre in Dublin. During the early 1920s, the company produced a series of new Scottish plays in Glasgow and, from 1927, they toured these plays throughout Scotland. During the 1920s, the Scottish National Players took on the character of an exclusive club, placing more and more restrictions on their membership and their activities. Its membership was confined to Glasgow's business and professional classes, so that – as one former member once put it – 'You almost needed a blood test before you got in' though there were one or two exceptions to the rule, including Archie Henderson, a Shotts miner, who joined the Scottish National Players while he was attending elocution and drama lessons in Glasgow. The Scottish National Players' productions reflect a similar social bias. They include a large number of Scottish history plays and a large number of contemporary dramas set in a rural and preferably Highland environment. They also include one or two plays about urban, middle-class life, but few (if any) present industrial working-class experience.

It was inevitable, then, that Joe Corrie and the Scottish National Players would clash and clash they did in the autumn of 1929, when Corrie contested the Scottish National Players' rejection of *In Time O' Strife*.

Corrie submitted a copy of *In Time O' Strife* to the three-man panel, which included Dr John McIntyre, alias John Brandane, the playwright and author of *The Glen Is Mine*; Dr O. H. Mavor, alias James Bridie, who was then about to embark on his playwriting career (his first play, *The Sunlight Sonata* was first performed by the Scottish National Players at the Lyric Theatre on 20 March 1928); and William Jeffrey, the Lepidus of this formidable triumvirate. The panel rejected *In Time O'*

*Strife* and returned the script to Corrie with various rec-
ommendations for improvement. Corrie revised the play
in accordance with these suggestions and re-submitted
it, whereupon it was rejected for a second time.

Naturally, Corrie was disappointed, but he accepted
the decision and maintained a relatively harmonious
relationship with the Scottish National Players, who
continued to act as agents for his published work
including *Hogmanay* and *In Time O' Strife* itself. Some
two years later, Corrie changed his mind and wrote to the
editor of *The Daily Record* and *The Glasgow Evening News*
newspapers, contesting the Scottish National Players'
rejection of his play. He made the decision to question
their judgement in the wake of the Scottish National
Players' production of Neil Gunn's play, *The Ancient
Fire*, presented at the Lyric Theatre on 8 October 1929.
Although the critics agreed that Neil Gunn showed
enormous potential as a writer, they condemned *The
Ancient Fire*'s lack of theatricality and went on to question
the Scottish National Players' competence to lead the
Scottish Dramatic Renaissance. One critic wrote:

> *The Ancient Fire* is a play that would never have been
> chosen by a judge of drama and in putting it for-
> ward for production the (Scottish National Theatre)
> Society have done the author a rank injustice. With
> any competence to recognise a play, they must have
> known it was undramatic . . . The Reading Panel
> have once again been misled by the lure of literature.
> They have not yet learned that the play must first
> of all be a play and that the literary consideration
> is a very minor affair – an impediment unless it is
> handled by a master of technique.

The critics' attitude to *The Ancient Fire* and to the Scottish
National Players themselves awakened Corrie's latent sus-
picions concerning the Scottish National Players' rejection
of *In Time O' Strife*. He too began to question the Scottish
National Players' judgement, their competence and their

impartiality and came to the conclusion that the Play
Reading Panel had rejected *In Time O' Strife* not because
it was a bad play, but because it was a socialist one.
Corrie's letter to the editor of *The Daily Record* and *The
Glasgow Evening News* argues that the Scottish National
Players rejected *In Time O' Strife* 'because they thought
it would not suit this Lyric audience of theirs, containing
they felt too much socialist propaganda'.

It would be difficult to prove that the Scottish National
Players rejected *In Time O' Strife* for political reasons.
The Scottish National Players Play Reading Panel and
their supporters wrote a great many letters of their own
to the editor of *The Daily Record* and *The Glasgow
Evening News* newspapers, in which they stuck to their
guns, arguing that *In Time O' Strife* lacked the literary
merit of *The Ancient Fire* 'as literature' and was, 'a piece
of ludicrous assumption on Mr Corrie's part'.

The Scottish National Players clearly had little or no
interest in Scottish industrial working-class life. At the
same time, their Play Reading Panel was extremely hostile
to political and, in particular, socialist drama.

James Bridie wrote to Corrie concerning Corrie's play,
*A Master of Men* in 1944:

> You have probably heard enough about politics. Put
> as much politics as you like into your next (if you
> want to!). I think you have advanced enough not to
> put in party clichés that everybody has heard and is
> dead sick of. Whatever his views, the only people
> who like them are mugs who cry when a drunken
> comedian sings about mother and exactly the same
> sort who used to cheer the Old Red, White and
> Blue. But I'm telling you! Only, it really is an
> infectious disease in left-wing writers.

Here, Bridie begins by affecting a tolerant attitude to
political drama but, by the end of the passage, we are in
little doubt that Bridie retains a certain fear of playwrights
who incorporate politics (an 'infectious disease') into their

plays and that he has nothing but contempt for the audiences who attend the productions of these plays.

That this battle is by no means over can be seen from a couple of brief quotations: one is from Alisdair Cameron, appointed by Professor Jan MacDonald to her Drama Department very recently: he writes:

In Scotland Corrie's major fight, Mrs Mackenney says, was with another 'establishment' group, the Scottish National Players. However, Corrie's struggle with them highlights an irreconcilable split in Scottish theatre between those who believed the soul of Scotland was to be found in the Highlands and in the folk tradition and those who believed that it was to be found in the political struggles of the industrial Lowlands. Later twentieth-century nostalgia for croft and craft has blurred this division. But the success of *The Cheviot, The Stag and the Black, Black Oil*, which tapped the race memory of the Clearances, showed that when the Scottish National Players chose to perform Neil Gunn's *The Ancient Fire*, a rather unwieldy experimental piece about the same subject, rather than *In Time O' Strife*, they were not completely misguided. Mrs Mackenney, in fact, provides ample evidence that not being performed by the Scottish National Players was the best thing that could have happened to *In Time O' Strife*, as it was then able to enhance its popular reputation by using the network of theatres, with a regular working-class audience, which the Scottish popular theatre could provide.

In the late 1940s, Bridie himself looked to the popular theatre to secure the reputation of the Citizen's which had not a huge success. He probably remembered the good use the Glasgow Repertory Theatre had made of Scottish vernacular drama, using the profits from *Wee MacGregor* to present Chekhov, Gorky and the work of some 30 Scottish playwrights. The Rep had also secured its local reputation by performing short plays to a large and mixed audience at the Alhambra and Bridie tried a similar tactic. This was the production of *The Tintock Cup*, which, while echoing the traditions of the Royal Princes' Theatre, managed to embrace the mythical with the Druids, the potent historical with Bonnie Prince Charlie and the instantly recognisable with the 'Hing', Tatty Bacchante and Battlin' Joe McClout. Had there been a real struggle between Bridie and Unity, *The Tintock Cup* would have been Battlin' Jimmie Bridie's *coup de grâce*, but this was not necessary because by 1950 Unity had, like many other successful Scottish amateur companies, destroyed itself.

So much for the end of cultural class-war!

In spite of the evasive language of his last sentence, Mr Cameron's attitude is very much in vogue today. It was *one* of the reasons for the Clydebuilt season.

After this season, which incidentally left 7:84 with considerable financial problems for the rest of the year, we planned to develop the work of the Company, and to make life more satisfying, by launching a sister-company, to be called General Gathering. After the undoubted popular and critical success of the Clydebuilt shows, we felt we could explore our heritage of popular culture from outside Scotland, broaden our, and our audience's concept of the possible, and at the same time make a permanent company who would have a variety of worthwhile things to do. Here's my optimistic proposal to the SAC:

1. General Gathering will have as its main function at present the great classics of world popular theatre, from Aristophanes via Shakespeare to Dario Fo, in such ways as to make them alive for a Scottish popular audience today.
2. By world popular theatre is meant that current of great theatre written primarily for the mass of people rather than a small, educated class or coterie.

There is no hard and fast line to be drawn, but the intention should be clear, and the final choice of play will depend on suitability for the audience and strong desire to do it, rather than on the niceties of history. The other main criteria for plays will be: (i) high literary value; (ii) potential for theatrical magic; and (iii) accessibility to the audience – by way of revelance, comedy, music, or some other connection with contemporary life and taste. Through our experience with popular audiences in 7:84, we feel confident that we are able to make these judgements, and to create the styles of presentation that will make those works accessible, indeed enjoyable to the people of Scotland.

3. By Scottish popular audience we mean primarily the non-theatre-goers, the working people of Scotland, the young people in school or on the dole, the people who make up the bulk of 7:84's audience on the road, but in the case of General Gathering, wider. General Gathering would go about finding this audience by designing their productions to tour to the heart of communities throughout Scotland, as well as to fill larger theatres in the cities. We would hope to create special relationships with certain areas, notably the Western Isles, Highland, Grampian, Lothian, Tayside and Strathclyde regions – while obviously not excluding others.

With the experience and contacts of 7:84 behind us, we feel that we are uniquely well placed to create an audience for these plays, and a service to this audience. We would expect it to be wider than the 7:84 audience in that we want General Gathering to play in schools, and to attract those who might not respond to 7:84's political position.

4. General Gathering will consist of a company of ten actors, five stage management/lighting/trucking people, one Administrator, one PR person, an Artistic Director, with secretarial and part-time book-keeping help.

Its work would be supervised by 7:84's Board of Directors, advised by a Specialist Advisory Group of educationalists, theatre historians, and representatives of the audience.

General Gathering will have a separate function and discipline from 7:84. It is not intended that the shows will have the same direct, interventionist political content as the usual 7:84 shows – which obviously does not mean that Aristophanes can be non-political! The main *political* purpose of General Gathering will be to recapture the history of popular theatre and re-present it to the people of Scotland. This is very different from, though related to, the work of 7:84, and obviously relates strongly to the Clydebuilt season in Glasgow.

On a theatrical level, we feel that 7:84 knows how to reach popular audiences, and can use this knowledge to bring the classics of popular theatre back to the audience they were written for. We would use directors who have worked with or learnt from the theatre of 7:84, and performers who will know how to reach the audience. The return benefit to 7:84 will be twofold; firstly it will give a greater diversity of experience to 7:84 company members, in every way, and secondly it will allow 7:84/General Gathering to hold together a company for a whole planned season of work, rather than from tour to tour.

In November '82 I sent this with a covering letter to the SAC:

I personally would want to commit myself whole-heartedly to this programme, and feel that it could be a development of major importance. I know there are many others who feel the same way.

I would stress that the confidence we have in the project comes from our experience of the audience response to the Clydebuilt season, which leads us to feel we could, with many of the same company work together, develop a lot further, keep the audience with us, and make a better contribution to Scottish theatre.

I have included also a budget for a straightforward 7:84

operation, with two shows of our usual variety touring for 20 weeks in the year. As you will see, we would really be looking for £146,000 to do this adequately – which is only £50,000 less than the combined budget. Of course, should your committee decide that General Gathering is a non-starter, then we would wish to proceed with 7:84's work. In this event, I personally would prefer to have a Guest Artistic Director for the year, and simply remain as unpaid Consultant and Chairman of the Board, should the Board so desire.

On this subject, however, I would like to say that should the combined 7:84/General Gathering project take off, I would want very much to remain as Artistic Director, but would ask our Board to appoint a new Chairman as soon as possible.

I am amazed that it is less than seven years since I wrote that confident blast; and that even then I was having doubts about continuing as Artistic Director of a dwindling output. The real situation by now with 7:84 was that overheads, the sheer cost of being in existence, were growing horrifically; and touring costs were going through the roof, and wages could not be kept down, nor should they have been, for the work we expected. We were lucky – outside the Clydebuilt year – if we could afford to mount two shows a year. If we wanted to go to the Highlands, we could afford a vestigial set and a tiny company only – as in *The Catch*, with five actors and a piano. There was also the fact that as we had a grant and paid above union minimum wages (just!), we should also pay overtime, and not expect any extra commitment from the actors without cash payments – though many did give huge amounts of time and effort from conviction. Around this time the union began to insist on no 'exploitation'.

All in all, 7:84 was becoming more of a management,

the company more of a work-force ranged against their 'bosses'. Because the company was not permanent – we could not afford it on existing finances – there were many 'hired hands', with short-term contracts. They were not involved in making decisions for the future work of the company, and they inherited the decisions of others about all the crucial areas of work. Company meetings, at which serious discussion should have been taking place, became occasions for the Administrator to wield power, i.e. to give out sets of instructions, and hand out the wages.

My own artistic planning was now having to be done earlier and earlier, to meet the demands of the Arts Council. The actors and others would have to be slotted into it at a later stage: the Taylorist work-ethic which we had tried to destroy by creating the company was being forced on us. Of course, I had a strong nucleus of actors, several of whom were on the Board of the company, whom I consulted at length, but this was not the same thing. The aim of that General Gathering plan was twofold: to allow us to introduce good, even great, popular theatre to Scotland, and to allow us to combine the extra income with 7:84 grant to form a permanent company again.

But we were in the 80s – even Scotland had to admit it was in Thatcher's 80s. My concern for the spiritual well-being of the company-members, for their playing a full part in deciding their own work, their own future, was alas not reciprocated. They wanted us to be bosses, and them to be fee-earning professionals. This is what I wrote soon after the event:

Following the critical success – and financial disaster – of Clydebuilt, I was very anxious to do two things to follow

it up. One was to put on a season of European plays –
taken up and improved upon by Mayfest. The other was
to try to create a structure for a much more permanent
company to present both new 7:84 plays and classics of
popular theatre, presented for 7:84 audiences.

The history of the idea of the company is easily
glossed over, and is important. In order to allow a
more genuinely democratic structure to emerge for the
company, and for that democracy to mean responsibility
as well as power to company members, it was obviously
necessary for them to commit themselves not just to one
show, but to the ongoing work of the company. The first
disappointment came when, at the instigation of Charlie
Kearney, a meeting of the nucleus of Scottish actors
and technicians called to discuss the project, voted for
a short-term rather than a long-term commitment. This
was understandable but not the point, and obviously
diminished the feeling of embarking on a big co-operative
venture.

The second disappointment came when three of the
four men called to that meeting pulled out of their
commitment without even a phone-call to say they were
doing so.

The third disappointment came when only two of the
women involved were prepared to commit themselves
beyond the Edinburgh Festival and tour. In short, the
original commitment that 7:84 and I were prepared to
make to an ongoing ensemble of actors, technicians and
administration was reduced to meaningless shreds by the
actors' lack of commitment.

Nevertheless we went ahead with a first project. The Arts
Council had *not* given us either an increase in our grant –
in fact it was cut by one per cent – or more than a small
'project' grant to do one show. It was not enough, but
fortunately the Official Edinburgh Festival under John
Drummond found the project interesting, and made a
contribution to production costs. It was still not enough

for a sensible budget for what we were trying to do; the company idea had collapsed; the Arts Council grant was far from a solution to our longer-term problems.

I should have resigned, and cancelled the show. I didn't do either, out of some insane optimism, and a passionate feeling that having won this small amount of cash for popular theatre, we had a duty to go on, not to give it back to the SAC. We had worked for 15 years to build a dialogue with a real, not a fake, working-class audience, and as a *writer* this was exactly the audience I wanted to work to.

But now the real strain was starting to come in the area of running the company, of the change in the nature of what could be achieved, the feeling that from now on I was required to spend more time, energy and worry on making ends meet for the company than in the comparatively joyful tasks of writing and directing plays.

Although we had had plays in the English 7:84 from a wide range of writers – like John Arden, Adrian Mitchell, Trevor Griffiths, and many others – nevertheless the company in Scotland was very much a part of my working life as a writer. I suppose I will lay myself open to some heavy criticism if I say this, but there is a sense in which the kind of company I wanted to keep on creating, writing and directing for, dedicating my life to, was not an institution at all: it was a family, a small working group of creative talents brought together by a common feeling for theatre and feeling for people and hope for society. At many stages in the story of both 7:84 companies we achieved great things through such close, creative groups, in which respect for each other released imagination, comedy, music, and commitment. Within those various groupings, usually either through being responsible for bringing them together, or through holding the pen, or guiding the research, or acting as director of the show, or through an accumulation of experience of policy-making and company management, I had been in some position of greater power or responsibility than most other individuals – but not than the collective, and not in areas where those individuals were specially skilled. So, to some extent, those groups were willing collaborators in my creative process, and I in theirs. I am aware of a touch of paternalism inherent in this, and would agree that anyway 'parentalism' was possible from time to time, but I have to say that I was conscious of this danger and constantly made aware of it by the others in the groups. The real point of this analysis however is that whatever their psychic structure, they were bonded by their size (never more than ten people), by familiarity, closeness, even intimacy, and by a shared love of what we were doing. In 1983, for me, that ended. It re-appeared only sporadically, and only with very small groups. Why?

I think I must confess that *real* directors like Peter Brook can generate this sense of intimate belongings and personal loyalty in huge numbers of people – actors, crew, PR people, crew at visiting venues, even large classes of other directors. And I have to say that I can't do this – I'm too much of a writer, too involved in what the thing is saying, to be able to project this kind of charisma. I need to work small, at least in small groups of people who trust each other and trust me, and from there we can go as big as anybody. It is a serious limitation in a director, and one I have become increasingly aware of.

I am beating my breast in this way because I think

the developments in 7:84 (Scotland) cannot be attributed solely to the workings of a consciously malign political force: many of them were, and some decisive ones were; but for the record, it must be said that this need for an atmosphere of trust and familiarity to work in, when denied or frustrated, has led me into many of the miseries and negative feelings that have marked the last five years, and have been my personal contribution to the downfall of 7:84 (Scotland). There have been other, greater, and more obnoxious contributions, but that was at the root of mine.

In a minute, when I come to some of the problems with the next show, we will see why I am raising this particular need, or limitation at this point. But I would like to examine its *unconscious* political construction and connections a little. The greatest happiness I had in working closely with a 7:84 company was in the way a collectively generated atmosphere of excitement, concern, anger, fun, wit, musicality, verbal play – a kind of theatrical sexuality – could generate scenes from me, performances, sets, costumes, from everyone, a production we all owned, and could then recreate itself nightly as a show and re-communicate that aura of intimacy, personal involvement, laughter and deep emotion to larger groups in halls and theatres all over Scotland or England or Holland or Dublin or Toronto or Leningrad: it was the fecundity of the inner workings of the ideas, words, music, people, of the event, that made itself felt and was valuable.

So although I say 'work small', I mean from this shows can grow that play to thousands at a time. And this sense of familiarity, of children listening to ghost-stories in tents, of knights in armour on kitchen tables, of a language of intimacy, is what lies I think at the heart of the appeal of popular culture, is what marks it off from the official, the national, the high culture of opera-house and RSC. It has many other features, of course, but maybe this is one which I have so far ignored, and which is central.

It was a quality I lost badly trying to make the next production. As I said, I should not have done it: not enough money, under-committed company, and an underfunded company operation. But it was Aristophanes, I had a great collaborator in my Greek friend and composer Thanos Mikroutsikos – and I wanted to do the show. I had started with the *Thesmophoriadzusae*, the story of the women of Athens dressing up as men, getting into the parliament before the men, and voting that as the men had made such a mess of things, the country should be run by the women. To this I added or interpolated a short, outrageous version of *Ippes, The Knights* in which the men respond by showing what happened when one particular woman came to power . . . They are driven off by the women, who have a big party, leaving some of the men quite happy to join in, others still stuck in sexist abuse: it was full of songs, terrible old jokes, and startlingly modern notions about the liberation of women. Of course Aristophanes was an old sexist mickey-taker, but as a writer he couldn't help himself – and where he went out of order, I had simply cut whole scenes, and/or replaced them with songs. On the whole, though, I was very close to the original. Let me give you what I noted a few weeks after the event:

What were we trying to do with these daft old pieces? Why revive them at all? The answer for me lies in the real subject-matter of Aristophanes. This is not so much in the 'political' area – though it connects, intimately – more in the really dangerous area of the unspoken – some would say unspeakable – areas of the collective psyche.

The fourth century BC in Athens produced a civilisation which – even though it had problems – has never been equalled in history. It produced works of art, plays, poetry, history, philosophy, that stand today as pinnacles of their genre. The real subject-matter, for me, of these plays was what Aristophanes was telling us about the state of the Athenian psyche that produced all this, and the huge gap which this reveals between our own consciousness and theirs.

All this, of course, in the context of comedy. And very old comedy at that. When the papers complained that the jokes were old, I was tempted to remind them that they were in fact 2,300 years old, and still doing quite well.

But it was the nature of the comedy that was going to reveal the profounder connections between the ancient Greek fertility and our contemporary Scottish aridity – if we had ever got to it.

From the beginning there was a huge built-in resistance within the company to this level of the play. In the production, I was asking the actors to explore this level. The connections between uninhibited play with cocks, shit, body-sweat, lust, erections, women's lusts and fantasies, body-hair, and all the bodily functions, – and the beautiful poetry that haunts the play, the magnificent boldness of the political and sexual-political ideas of the play, and the atmosphere of fruitful creativity in which the play was first made.

We never took this exploration beyond the first stages. Inhibition, fear, personal worries about being seen in public involved in this sort of thing, particularly among the majority of the women, even anger and shame, nipped the whole proceedings in the bud.

Because the major concentration of the play is on the women's psyches, and the main rehearsal problems lay in opening them up, the men grew restless and resentful of this unexpected lack of prioritisation. There was a demand for more attention to be paid to the men – and the women wanted to get on with blocking the piece, and to stop wasting time with this exploration, which they thought – perhaps all too correctly – would lead nowhere.

This created in me a sense of deep down failure even before we had properly begun. We never actually reached the level on which the production should have operated. I doubt if we ever could have.

All this was accompanied by a rather negative attitude in rehearsal. Bold strokes, experimentation, non-naturalistic inventiveness were openly laughed at, and mutual trust was destroyed. When the men did come into rehearsal with the women trying things out, the lack of support was embarrassing, the level of sexual politics a disgrace to a progressive company.

So the real subject-matter of the piece led to my trying to find things in the production which I failed, as a director, to release in the company. In my own defence I can only say that I doubt if anyone could have achieved this kind of release under the circumstances. The cast was suffering deeply from the very distance from the underside of the psyche that the rest of western Christian capitalist (or, at the moment, socialist) societies seem to be experiencing, and the same distance from the sources of Aristophanic comedy. Therein lay the source of most of my problems.

The net result of all this was that the production was imposed rather than discovered. I was unwilling to accept what seemed to be the direction in which the cast wanted to take the real meaning of the plays – and consequently was in some tension throughout. It would undoubtedly

have been easier to have simply accepted the suggestions
thrown up by the majority of the cast, but this would
have led to my remaining as director only in a cynical and
resentful way. So I tried my best to produce something
that would be nearer to the cast's sensibilities, but not
too far from my own sense of style.

The result was a major disaster. In August 1983 we
were due to open to the world's press in the Assembly
Rooms Music Hall on a Monday at 7.30. Due to ridiculous scheduling by the Assembly Rooms, we had grossly
inadequate time to get in and light. When we did, they
had made such a spaghetti of the lighting cables in the
roof, with far too many companies coming in, that we sat
up all Sunday night trying to find which plug came from
which lights. The company were called out at seven on
the Monday morning, and in mounting tension and fury
suffered a technical cock-up of the worst kind. By 6 p.m.
we still hadn't finished the lighting cues, the sound was
a disaster, and the company screwed up like snapping
fiddle-strings. At 7.30 we opened to an audience who
knew everything was wrong. Everything. The reviews
gloated over our shame, the Festival audiences stayed
away in their millions, and the cast were mutinous.
They held a meeting in Glasgow to which I was not
invited, and came to a full company meeting armed
with resolutions.

The main problem was ostensibly that the 7:84 Board
saw that if we continued to tour the show we would
probably lose over sixteen thousand pounds. If we took
it off immediately and paid everyone their full fees
it would lose only three thousand pounds: so they
decided we must take it off. If not, we could not
proceed with the autumn show, and would end up
in great money problems which would give the SAC

a reason to close us. It was a deeply unhappy time, and one that I don't care to repeat. At the full company meeting, various members of the cast said they had told me so in rehearsal, that the men had better lines than the women, that Aristophanes 'had not written a socialist or a feminist play', that the part Liz MacLennan played was more positive only because she was my wife, and that this was a problem too, creating exclusivity, and that basically it was all my fault. The company's main anger was that the show was coming off. They wanted it to continue, and felt 7:84 was being paternalistic in ignoring their wishes, even though they would not be affected by the cancellation of the next show, and would of course be paid in full for the whole tour. At that meeting I vowed I would never again direct actors in the theatre in Scotland, being unable to cope with their attitudes, and feeling unable to communicate with the majority of the company or elicit an imaginative response. On the whole, I stuck to this vow until I left 7:84, and it has had very serious consequences for the company.

What it all boiled down to was a basic lack of respect, trust, love, fellow-feeling, shared joys or shared concerns. Something had happened to that generation of actors under the new regime at the Glasgow drama school – founded by James Bridie – and it was something that broke my whole way of working. The spirit of Thatcher's 80s was getting through to me where it really did damage.

From then on, my relationship with 7:84 (Scotland) was very different. I concentrated on producing rather than directing, and in fact did far less writing for the company. I also spent a lot of time making television versions of *Blood Red Roses* and a new Highland show, *There is a Happy Land*, and of course during 1984/85 had to cope with the high dramas in London with the ending of the active life of 7:84 (England). Other, non-artistic duties began to weigh heavily. One administrator had identified a particular deficit as 'nearly £8,000'. As she discovered over the months that it was in fact £36,000 we grew concerned over this startling margin of error. We had to go dark for five months. She resigned, but later got a lawyer to take her case to ACAS for wrongful dismissal, on the basis that we had not offered her her job back when we began work again. We could have fought it, but the propaganda damage to the left-wing company of being sued by an ex-employee would have made many a pressman's day – we went through hoops, but ended up having to pay, even though we would have won. Blackmail of a political kind is not unknown, but the whole process took time, effort, and money we didn't have. Another administrator stayed for a year, then left for a better-paid job. The next one drove me mad, having come from a VAT office, with I'm afraid a decided tendency to crush any creativity out of me at least, though I'm sure those who loved her found the opposite. I began to avoid going into the office more than was absolutely necessary. Her assistant administrator sat for a year or so, 'doing the books' – apparently a full-time job. When he left, we discovered the petty cash had not been 'done' for six months, and was in chaos; it cost more money to have it done. In June 1985 I did write to the Board offering my resignation. At that time, I wrote:

> If the SAC come up with another standstill grant next year, or worse, – we could end up with even less small-scale and Highland touring.
>
> As it is, we have had to abandon the planned follow-up to *The Albannach*, which should have been for next

spring, and to abandon thoughts of an autumn tour this year. The play we have commissioned from Sean McCarthy will have to be shelved indefinitely, and the prospect of mounting a Christmas Show fell through because it was totally dependent on raising co-production money – not enough of which was forthcoming.

The £70,000 plus earmarked for overheads is now firmly committed and there is no chance of making any of it available for production in the current year. It will go towards wages of administrators with nothing to administer, and a production manager with no productions, and offices, accounting, insurance, vehicles etc. with no great purpose.

As Artistic Director, I have cancelled my retainer from the end of May as I am working with Freeway on *Blood Red Roses* through the summer, but I see no point at all in coming back on the pay-roll with no prospect of any art to direct.

I propose that it should be our urgent task to reduce the overheads from 60% of our grant to more like 20%, and to liberate the rest of the money for what we should be doing – putting on shows and touring them.

The net result of all this is:

1. The company finds itself pretty well totally dependent on one source of funding – a source which has a habit of dwindling, and is in no way permanent, or necessarily permanently well-disposed, as 7:84 (England) discovered.
2. This apparent lack of foresight and effort in the broader sweep of the company's general management, when combined with the results of management decisions over the past few years on the imbalance between overheads and production money, has resulted in a disastrous situation for the company.
3. Out-dated and time-wasting procedures and Luddite attitudes towards automation seem certain to perpetuate this situation.

4. And yet there seems to be an inability to recognise the gravity of the situation, and a deep reluctance to do anything about it on the part of the same administration which led us here.

It seems to me that the Board should now really consider its options, and take more responsibility for the future.

I lay out here some options for consideration. They may appear hard, but they are not as drastic as some others which are not suggested.

The company began its life, and continues, as a theatrical organisation working very consciously in the context of class struggle in a class society – hence the name, the perspective, and the practice of the company.

However, the nature of the class struggle changes in large lurches – both backwards and forwards. We are in the middle of recovering, very slowly, from a series of major defeats for the working-class. The resistance movement that we are part of is very different from the revolutionary upsurge that we were part of when we began. What I think we must learn is that history has not stood still, nor will it.

We have gone through a classic period of looking to our roots, of building basic working-class self-awareness, of building more solid relationships with the rest of the movement. My fear is that if we continue the way we are, two consequences will follow:

1. We will be unable to move on from our present posture. It is already time to rethink. We are settling into old orthodoxies, and as usual paranoia and inertia come into play to keep us there.

2. We will lose the creative, open and if necessary dangerous atmosphere in which proper rethinking can happen. I personally think that huge sections of the labour movement are in this difficulty. It should be our role to enter fearlessly into such developments, not hide behind them.

The other consequence is that ways of working, and the relations of productions keep on changing faster than we can keep up with them. If we are to remain in the same decade as our audience, we must move faster, and use what developments there have been, not ignore or simply decry them.

It could well be that the place for me to indulge such notions is not 7:84 as it now is. This could well be, and I will accept that if necessary. One thing I cannot accept is continuing in the present groove.

That was part of a report I made to the Board in June 1985. By the time I had finished writing it, I was also seriously offering my resignation:

Dear Fellow Board Member,

The enclosed document originated as a series of radical proposals to help deal with what I saw as an impossible situation for 7:84. It has unfortunately ended as a letter of resignation from my role as Artistic Director of 7:84 (Scotland).

Talking about my own survival as a writer is not something I do a great deal, but it has something central to do with my offering my resignation at this time.

As will be apparent from the contents of the rest of this letter, 7:84 (Scotland) is in both a strong position, and in a weak position. I believe it is strong artistically, but very weak in that its structures have become ponderous, and for other reasons I outline below.

I find it difficult to continue as Artistic Director with the problems I speak of, and find that the danger is that the only way I could resolve the situation would mean giving up writing anything at all in order to do so.

This led to a long and very distressed Board meeting, which ended with my resignation being accepted. Under any other business, the Administrator announced, after three hours of self-justifiction, or attack, as the best form of defence, that she had been offered a much better-paid job, and would let us know the next day whether she was going to accept it or not. I was amazed at this, and after a lot of pressure from the Board, agreed to re-think my position if we could find a new and dynamic and positive administrative set-up. We didn't, but I stayed on. I shan't go into more detail, suffice it to say that at few points during those years did I, as Artistic Director, feel relaxed and confident about the actual management of the company. It was a nightmare, and made more so by the SAC's constant demands for weekly returns, daily returns, hourly returns – and their primitive reaction to not getting enough paper. Finally, they forced me to appoint to the Board a whizz-kid, a businessman, who ran a successful medium-sized concern, mostly selling motor-bikes to teenagers.

Trying to embrace the spirit of the 80s, we made him Chairman of our Finance Committee; then with strong pressure from the SAC (charmingly applied), we made him Chairman of the Board. He applied the rules for making profit from motor-bikes to the making of socialist theatre. Within a year he had allowed the SAC to take our annual grant away, after a series of meetings with them at which I was not allowed to be present.

Those events are all too close for me to write an objective narrative at the moment. Looking back on the whole history of 'the office', it is clear that once the running of the company's affairs was removed from company discussion, a Board set up to employ an administrator responsible to it for 'professional' management, then the whole enterprise of 7:84 was doomed. 7:84

was an attempt to create new structures, new ways of relating within a company, new and flexible ways of deploying our resources most effectively in a theatrical and political struggle. Once we had accepted specialisation in *management*, then we were subject to normative pressures, we became more and more like everybody else. But because we *weren't* like everybody else, we had huge problems. The Arts Council, who had forced this inappropriate structure on us in the interests of business efficiency, was run by administrators. Naturally they came down heavily on the side of the administrators they had imposed on us, and attacked me for 'failing to keep good administrators', which was their constant complaint. Finally, under enormous pressure, we were obliged to break our 17-year-old rule that nobody in the company is paid more than anyone else. We took on a tough, ruthless, administrator who had worked for several years at the Royal Court in London, to come in and rescue the company, at a salary more than twice that of everyone else. I'm sure the trains now run on time. I left, last July, finally and decisively.

The final straw came when the SAC, having announced in March 1989 that it would withdraw our revenue grant, then agreed to reconsider 'if it felt sufficient changes had been made'. These changes were in the areas of the Board, the administration and artistic policy. I shall return to Artistic policy, and have told you the solution to the adminstration problem. The final straw was that I was supposed to write to people who had supported the company since we began, to those long-standing members of the company who were on the Board, to people who put on and promote our shows from all over Scotland, to political supporters and old friends like Norman Buchan and Gordon Brown, and ask them to leave the Board now, to make way for businessmen, lawyers, accountants, PR men, fund-raisers and people who were not so supportive politically – people who were, in the immortal words of the SAC – 'objective'. This stuck in my throat. To sack Gordon Brown because he rarely got to meetings in Edinburgh was silly. To sack the people who gave us our strength in the communities was sickening. I pointed out that this condition was blatant political interference in the policy-making body of the company. They had nothing to say, shrugged their shoulders. The New Realism had sunk its teeth into my work, and was not going to let go. They of course had absolute power over our resources. Again I felt that we should try to rescue our money for *something* for our audiences. This time it meant I should go, not stay. I wrote to the new Chairman of the Board (the whizz-kid having done his work and left), and resigned, but I'm still, for the time being, on the Board.

All this rambling on about administrators and Boards and structures may sound like a huge diversion, a discrete set of problems which should be solved efficiently in their own world; but it's hard to hand over the running of the company to a Board and a Manager when you are trying to change the whole set-up. However, for a time, after *Women in Power*, I tried to do just that. Never mind how it gets there, I tried to tell myself, what matters is what goes on the stage. And, for sanity's sake, that is where my concentration went.

I proposed a six-part strategy. There would be three main and three subsidiary areas of our work. In November 1987 I had to write a Three-Year Plan for the Arts Council. In it I tried to sum up these areas, and mention briefly some of the shows in each, in answer to a question on 'general policy'.

## SAC Three-Year Plan, Question 5.

5. Please state briefly your organisation's long-term aims and objectives and the policies you employ to reach them.

The long-term policy of 7:84 remains what it has always been: to take theatrical entertainment of the highest quality to the traditionally non-theatre-going public – the working classes, the unemployed, the disenfranchised – wherever it is accessible to them, usually to where they would naturally go for an evening's entertainment, and to draw them into a dynamic relationship with theatre by creating it about their lives, their concerns and history and aspirations, and by telling the story in ways that are culturally familiar to those audiences. At the same time, to re-examine those cultural traditions critically. In short to provide a good night out – with a redefinition of that concept. This policy is both a political one and an artistic one, springing both from an identification with the political needs of our audiences, and from a desire on the part of those involved in the company to find a way to make theatre that speaks to their own class, without having to translate it into the language of the average Barbican-goer.

The company has identified up to this point three main areas of work and three subsidiary areas of work, and has structured itself accordingly. The three main areas of work are:

1. Large/medium-scale tours: these have been of very popular shows either of our own creation, or recoveries from the past, and have been directed by Giles Havergal and more recently by David Hayman. David is now Associate Director of the company. These shows have originated often in Mayfest, and gone on to tour the major theatres of Scotland, with great success.

2. Highland tours: the company has enjoyed a huge complicity with Highland audiences ever since *The Cheviot, The Stag and the Black Black Oil*, and the dialogue is still vibrant and ongoing. There have been three strands of this work recently: the adaptation of Highland classics like *The Albannach*, to be followed soon by *The Silver Darlings*; the musical shows, like *There is a Happy Land*, where the emphasis is on the story told through music; and the narrative-polemical, like *The Catch*, or recently *Mairi Mhor*. It should not be too readily assumed that one of these strands is more popular or more fruitful than the others.

3. Small/medium-scale tours: in the last five years Ian Wooldridge, David MacLennan, Finlay Welsh, Sandy Neilson, John McGrath and more recently John Haswell have directed a succession of shows playing in the parts where other theatre can't reach; in clubs, halls, unemployment centres, community centres, as well as small theatres, and in some cases extending the run into the larger theatres and off to tours in England, and further afield.

The company values these three areas of work, and intends to continue to develop them.

The main areas of development, apart from that sought in the large/medium scale, will be an increasingly careful selection of the venues to ensure that they will draw crowds that will justify either in income or other ways the visit of the company, and the expense involved. The days of experimental trips to Eriskay may well be over. We shall be looking more and more for strong evidence of local support.

The three subsidiary areas of the Company's work are as follows:

1. Publications and records: the company has seen as part of its overall policy the need to publish several of the plays it has produced, and associated material. The plays of John McGrath which it has published

are now out of print, and have made their investment back with a considerable profit. The Clydebuilt
season saw the recovery of many remarkable plays.
As well as performing them ourselves, we saw it as
part of the job to make them available to others, and
so we have now published three excellent volumes of
these works, and are about to launch an overview of
Popular Theatre in Scotland this century, by Linda
MacKenney, whom we involved in research at a very
early stage.

We will continue with this publication policy. It
is both part of our artistic work, and a source of
income. Similarly, our early records are now sold
out, and we have gone into partnership with a small
commercial record producer to bring out Catherine-
Ann MacPhee's first album, which has already paid
its cost and is into a small profit. We will continue to
produce suitable records when the funds build up.

2. Community work: John Haswell has joined us, after
an attachment as Arts Council Trainee Director, and
has considerable ability in the field of animating
community work – as well as being an excellent
director. Feeling we need to build stronger and more
lasting links with the communities we play in, we
have asked John to begin a series of community
workshop schemes, whereby the theatrical skills of
the company can be passed on to those who are keen
to learn in selected working-class and country
communities. The first of these was in Gorgie in
Edinburgh, and was a great success. John has recently
been involved in another scheme based on this in
Shetland. We will continue and develop this line of
work.

3. International tours and special events: this side of
the work has been of great value and interest, and
will continue, but, we hasten to add, at no cost to
the SAC.

Having outlined briefly these areas, we must add the other

new area mentioned earlier – the series of promenade and open-staged shows which we are now looking for a space to develop. The details will be evident in the future plans section, but suffice it to say that the intention is to break ground in staging, to bring a new dynamic to audience relationship, and to bring a much greater awareness of design, colour and new patterns of movement than we have shown in the past.

Another important policy feature has been that we have always found new audiences through the nature of our work and the way we market it. We want to increase the efficiency of our marketing, without losing the contact with organisations of all kinds who have helped us in the past. We all will spend more now on conventional publicity methods than we have in the past.

We believe that our audiences are ready for a lot more work with the same basic principles, but are ready for new adventures in style and performance.

We have arrived in the Age of the Administrator. In every walk of public life, from Cambridge professors' pay-scales to housing benefit to unemployed teenagers, ever greater power is being handed to the race of *apparatchiks* known as Administrators. A leading surgeon told us recently that the new values of cost-effectiveness and competition being implanted by the government in the Health Service were leading him and his colleagues towards a 'work to rule' attitude. 'If I did only the number of hours per week written in my contract, I'd be finished for the week by Wednesday! But what would happen to patients on Thursday and Friday? They would have to be treated by the Adminstrators!'

The imposition of controls, rules of competition, constant evaluation, the assessment of conformity to the Thatcherite ideology, the permanent threat of 'cost-effectiveness' exercises, are all instruments of the will of this government. Their implementation has led to the creation of an administrative bureaucracy with enormous power reminiscent of that of Czarist Russia.

So much for the diminution of 'state' power.

# 5

# Standards, Values, Differences

In the last two weeks I tried to talk a little about the importance of sustaining a plurality of cultures in the world, and I tried to outline some of my own experience in Scotland to show some of the possibilities, problems and difficulties of working in sub-cultures outside the mainstream during the 80s.

The questions I would like to raise today are related to this experience, and are to do with value. I believe the Cambridge English faculty has historically placed a certain emphasis on evaluation, the establishment of a 'canon' of English literature, a hierarchy of goodness and badness with inexact criteria fought over and rejected every decade or so. This is all very entertaining stuff, unless you're in it, I imagine, but it rarely impinges on the debates of Arts Council advisory committees, nor does it sell many theatre tickets. People on the Left also have a certain caution about 'evaluation' – for the good reason that it can lead to élitist attitudes, hierarchies, and, when negative, can crush good things before they have a chance to develop. Nevertheless it seems to me most important to the health of a theatrical culture that some thought should be given to the larger questions of why some things are worth encouraging and others have to be neglected.

In the present climate in Britain almost the sole criterion seems to be the ability to raise money – either by a pimping populism or compliance with the desires of a sponsoring business's PR strategy. The other criteria are: internal business efficiency and the ability to write impressive reports backed with figures, pie-charts, and yuppie prose. In amongst this pandering to the market and the 'enterprise culture', the criteria by which artistic and social value-judgements are made are treated as painfully obvious, as susceptible to the same bluff, common-sense aggressive assertions as is, say, the need for a royal family.

When there are, as occasionally there are, heart-searching sessions on 'priorities', the values of the arts establishment are usually not artistic. 'Provision' is one key-word, meaning the creation of a set of pre-packed institutions in a large city in a region, 'providing' arts fare for the arts-lovers of the region. There is talk of 'extending provisions', i.e. bussing in school parties from the periphery to the centre, of merrily carting a cheaper version of the approved product from the centre to bits of the periphery. What it actually is, is usually described as 'of a high standard'.

'Excellence' is the other key-word of the new domineering ideology. What is 'excellent' about a piece of work is rarely – and only vaguely – defined. Lord Mogg is fond of 'excellence', but has as far as I know, failed to produce a definition or a description of it, clearly believing it to be self-evident.

In music, of course, criteria are a little easier – if a musician plays the wrong notes, or the wrong tempi, we can tell. In dance, competence is usually physically apparent. In theatre, art and poetry the basic levels of skills are fairly obvious also, but operate at such a low level that they are virtually meaningless. 'Excellence' as it is used in theatre, seems to relate to the reputation of the stars and the director, the size of the budget, the power of the publicity machine, and the consensus of a group of white, male, middle-class theatre critics. Of course a famous play or author enhances the excellence, and gives a sort of moral guarantee, and the consistency of the theatre in producing such 'excellence' is a further aid to the connoisseur. Perhaps the ultimate criterion is international recognition: so Peter Hall by powerful diplomacy and lobbying has his *Oresteia* put on at Epidavros, and it is terrifically excellent. What the Greeks thought of it – and several have spoken about it – does not matter.

Of course, somewhere along the line, some thoughts about the actual shows are at work. The director will be saying: 'How can I make this excellent?' If he, it is usually a he, is in Leeds Playhouse, he'll want it to be excellent so he can get a better job with the RSC. If it's at the Traverse, he or she will be wanting a different kind of excellence to impress the talent-spotters of the Royal Court, or Hampstead. The designer will be wanting the photos of the set (or the model) in *Theater Heute* so they'll get an opera in Hamburg, and the writer, if alive, will be hoping for excellent notices to launch the play into international orbit, and his or her career into the big time, with movies and the chance to write a libretto for Andrew Lloyd Webber. Excellence matters.

But what exactly is it?

I'm afraid I'm not in a position to tell you, having been cut several times by the arts establishment for not being excellent enough – indeed for not even aiming at this common-sense excellence.

I can tell you perhaps which new plays, or their authors are 'excellent'. Tom Stoppard, for example, is unbelievably excellent; the characteristics most admired being cleverness, wit, sophistication, cynicism, and the ability to vulgarise a few strands of recent philosophy. Politically well to the right, bitterly anti-Communist, refusing to boycott South Africa, and very unwilling to talk about any of these, Stoppard is therefore reticent, as befits a 'non-political' writer, and right-wing at the same time. David Hare, the left-wing equivalent, is not so clearly excellent, and has not a few problems, being fortunate in having friends to fight for him. Howard Barker is the new Crown Prince of excellence, making a virtue of difficulty and ambivalence. He writes: 'The theatre must start to take its audience seriously. It must stop telling them stories they can understand.' This is going in the right direction for excellence, or a season at the RSC. Barker also writes some very intelligent and important things about the authoritarian in the theatre – left as well as right – with which I heartily agree. But this sort of intellectual arrogance is the tool of the sub-Stoppard, the weapon of the people who would rather have the audience *not* know what is being said, but vaguely feel it to be important.

I don't wish to attack my colleagues personally, but they are in their work contributing to a mythology of excellence which I cannot endorse.

I have, earlier in these talks, tried to outline some different criteria for evaluating a piece of theatre. Outside the mainstream of bourgeois theatre – which I do not dismiss – I have pointed to the need for a whole layer, across the country, of a rich, thriving, popular theatre, a theatre which connects with groups of people rather than nations, which grows from the traditions of popular entertainment, rather than from misapplied modernism – a theatre that calls on the long-suppressed sub-cultures of the working classes rather than the inflated achievements of high culture – a pre-modernist rather than a post-modernist creativity.

I would like to now leap again into my own fumbling attempts to encourage this, and to give you some idea of the huge task this is – but also some of the joys of partial success.

Let me go back to 7:84 (Scotland), and give some idea of how we were thinking and working over the last few years. I have talked about the painful administrative and organisational and financial problems – let me now look at the artistic area, and where our value-judgements led us into conflict with those of the consensus.

Last November I wrote the Three-Year Plan for the SAC which I cited last week. I'd like to give you one more passage from it. They ask:

6. *Please list your main goals over the next three years and briefly describe your plans for implementing them.*

It has been counter-productive to try to separate this question from the previous question. However:
By the end of a three-year period we aim to see the company working from a base in Glasgow with rehearsal, workshop, wardrobe, store and office all under one roof, with the possibility of performing in this space – but without responsibility to run a new venue – and with an identification with another performance space of a less conventional nature. The company will be taking out first-rate tours to the smaller- and medium-scale venues in the industrial areas, to the halls of the Highlands and Islands, to new spaces in the big towns which are not conventional theatre spaces, and with

a constant output of large- and medium-scale theatre pieces.

We will be publishing a series of plays, theatre-studies and associated books, and producing tapes and records of a high quality that will be generating a sizeable contribution to our income. We will be involved in the television presentation of two out of three of our shows, and will be touring widely through the world when not touring Scotland. We will have a flourishing programme of community work under way, and be in demand for this work all over Scotland and elsewhere. We will be introducing new companies from abroad to Scotland, and will be bringing distinguished directors to work with Scottish actors and sending our directors to work abroad.

The main plans for implementing these goals are: to raise more income from a variety of sources; to pursue the idea of the move to Glasgow and the search for a good space and help of all kinds from Glasgow District; to strengthen the administrative team to cope with the work-load, and to pay them better; to push on more vigorously with the most exciting schemes that we already have under way.

I hope it is clear how this artistic strategy fits in with the general principles of our analysis of the importance of class-consciousness, popular culture in its diversity, and ultimately the question of the role of the state. Audience size grew dramatically over these years, particularly in Glasgow and in the Highlands.

Having refused, after *Women in Power*, to direct Scottish actors in theatre, I was delighted to give David Hayman the chance to direct a string of very Glaswegian big theatre shows, which he did with some success, opening them in Mayfest, touring to all the major theatres, and still managing some important small venues. The Highland shows were my province, and here audiences grew in most places, and the shows were close to people's lives, and meant a lot to them. In the industrial area small-scale touring we had a few problems. Quite a few of the shows – not all – were not very well done, and anyway there was a new set of demands in these areas that a company with a big band, rock'n'roll and forthright politics like Wildcat were able to satisfy much better than we were. In this area we made serious mistakes.

I did direct some Scottish actors – I made an exception for Liz MacLennan, with whom I've worked for 17 years, and for whom I wrote a one-woman show about George Orwell, Central America and US power, called *The Baby and The Bathwater*. Carlos Arredondo, a Chilean living in Edinburgh, provided the music for this, and it was the nearest I came personally during this time to a satisfying attempt to grapple with the complexities of the mid-80s. It found a lot of response in Scotland, on an English tour, in pit-head canteens during the miners' strike, and in Canada. The form was another development – a cross between ceilidh and *diseuse* – but it essentially used very fragmented pieces of evidence to challenge the audience to make leaps, to piece together a polemic. It used old Chilean Indian songs and Orwell parody, Edinburgh school-girl and GI thug, a woman bureaucrat in London and Rigoberta Menchu, who was a Quiche Indian who wrote vividly of her experiences in Guatemala, all in a rup-tured series of disjunctions, demanding correlation by the audience. It was an attempt to link the mind of a young Scots girl to the ideology that produced it, and the other ghastly realities which that ideology sup-ports. It was about 'national' as well as 'popular', and about connections and discontinuities. In some ways it returned to a preoccupation of some of my earlier plays, with moral evasion, the ease of slipping out of responsibility for terrible things, the eel of the English conscience. In other ways, it opened up new territory, in its kaleidoscopic structure and its systems of reference across decades and continents. I don't know how brilliant it was to others, but it felt exciting to me. And, incidentally, it raised a lot of money for the miners, for the Guatemala Commission for Human Rights, and it sold quite a few copies of Rigoberta's book.

But all this effort was made doubly difficult. The 'administrative' set-up, as described last week, constantly undermined the work, and demanded more and more attention. In the bad old days it was the stars, or the director or the writer whose temperaments had to be cossetted. Now it is the delicate vanity of the administrator which we must make our first priority. They now have the power, and the ego-trip, and the highest wages – the stars are nowhere. If you are prepared to sit in an office and do a fairly simple piece of organising with regularity and application, you've got power: you don't need to be able to add up, you can hire a book-keeper. More seriously, the finances in 86/87 began to go desperately wrong, and left a deficit that gave the SAC their chance: clear it, in one year, or we'll cut you. Although in 87/88 we reduced it by nearly £16,000 it was not cleared. It was one of their main reasons for cutting us.

The other difficulty is more complex, and begins to relate to the question of values, provision and excellence. The SAC Drama Committee is composed of the worthy and the pliant from several walks of life: in the late 80s it has included various professors, a Gaelic playwright with pretensions, a mediocre poet, a teacher from Bridie's Drama School, a headmaster, a BBC producer, a bureaucrat, an actor who resigned, a writer and a director who felt unable to cope with it, and a theatre administrator or two.

A story might illustrate the class orientation of this lot. The poet, no doubt of working-class origins, writes poems in a funny, lovable Glasgow dialect, the most famous of which is about the coming of some identifiably working-class hooligans whom he sees as in a nightmare threatening to invade his psychic space. At a meeting with the SAC he chided me for not employing a wider spread of Scottish writers: I pointed out that few would bother to commit themselves to our audiences, being more intent on Broadway via the Royal Court (e.g. John Byrne, who is at least open about it). He poo-pooed this notion: 'What would you say to a writer who you wanted to commission?' he demanded. I replied that I'd remind them they were taking part in an ongoing dialogue with a working-class audience in, say, Clydebank Town Hall. He looked aghast. 'Why should a writer have to write *down* in that way?' he said. Down. That is what he said – write down. I became angry and offered to throw him out of the room. I was restrained by my administrator. The Arts Council chairperson and officials were a little awkward about this revealing slip of the poetic persona, but said no more, tried to change the subject. I am no longer Artistic Director of 7:84. In March 1988, when our notice went out, this particular poet was still on the Drama Committee.

The Chairman of this Committee at the time was an academic, and, like James Bridie, a staunch member of the board of the Citizen's Theatre. She rose surprisingly easily to the Chair of Drama at Glasgow University. She is renowned for her 'international' approach – and her down-grading of the importance of new Scottish writing.

Glasgow is in Scotland, and therefore, it is felt in some quarters, that its citizens will want, will need, and certainly ought to have Scottish drama performed by Scottish actors directed by Scottish directors. To declare my prejudices at the outset, I believe that what I term, facetiously, the haggis hunt for the great new Scottish play has been the bugbear of the development of the theatre in Scotland. I understand the sensitivity to cultural domination in a nation that has been for so long administered politically from elsewhere. I understand that cultural domination is insidious and is transmitted too easily and perhaps unwittingly by educational means. I also accept that in some cases a play that talks about Sauchiehall Street rather than the Strand, or one set in Helensburgh rather than in Haslemere, can have more immediate relevance to a Scottish audience, but I cannot agree that the theatre in Scotland owes any Scottish playwright a living, or that any form of positive discrimination should be adopted in favour of Scottish writers. The best way to establish a healthy school of playwrighting in Scotland is to introduce the writers to as many of the best foreign plays as possible produced as well as possible: French, German, American, Russian – and even English.

If we are to assume that a particular Scottish character exists, one that demands a Scottish dramatist to express it, we must determine what it is. I offer to you the comment of the critic, Hazlitt, who remarked that the Irish character was in his view much more adapted for the stage than was the Scottish. The Scottish character depends, he says, on a calculation of consequences, just as in the Scottish accent 'every syllable is held fast between the teeth, and kept in a sort of undulating suspense, lest

circumstances should require a retraction before the end
of the sentence'. This was hardly, he suggested, the
temperament or the speech for the theatre. Far be it from
me to suggest that the Scots are, by nature, untheatrical
– their skill in rhetoric and delight in disputation would
instantly refute it – but I believe that we have more
in common with people of other races than we have
differences from them. There is no doubt at all that
a Glasgow citizens' theatre should mount productions
that are meaningful to a Glasgow audience, however
that audience might be composed, but that does not
necessarily mean a diet of plays by Scots or about
Scotland. Such parochialism will never give us our own
National Theatre and it is, paradoxically, a product of the
very cultural insecurity from which we seek to escape.

Her values are precisely those of the 'centres of excellence' concept that has destroyed a whole sector of
English theatre, and represent the Scottish branch of
multi-national culture industry. Politically she denies
being a Tory – but she cannot grasp the politics of
culture, either class or national. As a would-be actress
she may think she understands the inner workings of
theatre, but the only theatre she understand is bourgeois
theatre, and everything else, like 7:84, she dismisses as
'variety'.

Her Committee, guided by its Drama Director and
Drama Officer, are charged with helping to build a rich
web of theatre culture in Scotland, and make it available
to all of the people, whoever and wherever they may be.
They do spread a small amount of money very thinly
but with great noise to send out grossly under-funded
tiny groups, some not even of Equity members, so they
can stick pins on the map of the Highlands and the
Borders.

What is centrally at issue is that they cannot perceive

any cultural distinctiveness, any need for relating to popular culture. As my successor as Artistic Director of 7:84 said, if they enjoy a show in Glasgow, why should they 'be denied' that show in the Hebrides? There is a very long answer to that question.

The assessors working to this committee brought in a series of reports on our work which reveal the same refusal to understand. They also reveal a hostility to our work which I found shocking. They represent the ideological operation of the capitalist state in as pure a form as I have encountered. The role of the 'organic intellectual' in cultural hegemony writ large, the connection between the intellectual climate and the material means of production as in a diagram.

Last summer, in the village I spend my time in in the Highlands, there came to the village hall a thing about clowns – a group of what my children call hippies, in an old bus. They were far from professional, and did a thing that nowhere touched a scrap of relevance or contact with people's lives: they came with a grant from the SAC. This year it is being increased. In Skye, I saw a silly middle-class novel about a monster (with a lot of crude fun about the locals) playing to a middle-class audience in Portree – again with a large grant from the SAC. Of course I do not wish to stop either of these activities: but the SAC have stopped ours – which were rooted in the lives, language and history of the Highland people. My last show, about Mairi Mhor MacPherson, a great woman of Skye and Glasgow in the 1880s, who began to write songs when she was 50 and produced wonderful lyrics, big songs – was made yet another reason for cutting 7:84. What was interesting was the values inherent in the SAC's assessment of it:

Mairi Mhor is not highly thought of in Gaelic academic circles as a poet but Sorley MacLean has her better: he loves her for her 'great heart'. Mairi wrote and sang songs to inspire the crofters' struggle for the land at the end of the nineteenth century . . .

Her story provides rich material for dramatisation. We want to get to the core of this big lady with the 'great heart', who, at radical meetings, sang her own songs, created in response to the political realities of the moment. We want to discover the hidden springs of her inspiration; her agonised sense of the injustice done to her that burned and responded to the sense of injustice felt by the landless crofters.

We get very little of this in *Mairi Mhor: Woman of Skye*. We are indeed *told* part of her story. But telling is not drama. Only the singing of her songs by Catherine-Ann MacPhee prevented the play from boring the audience. The grafting on of some material about Nicaragua today was both idiosyncratic and puzzling. We learn almost nothing of Mairi as a person because the material about her is presented in undigested chunks. Only Big Mary's songs make an impression and the play is little more than a ceilidh of her songs, joined together by some polemical narration.

Audience of 600–700, virtual capacity, were polite and faithful to 7:84, but I felt were not moved or fully satisfied by this performance.

He omits to mention the standing ovation these 6–700 people gave the show, the tears in the eyes, the appeals to 'come back soon'.

What emerges from an overall examination of these anonymous assessments – some clearly written by our friend who feels he can't write 'down' to the workers – is a fairly incoherent, unthought-out set of ideas about what 'theatre' should be. 'Telling is not drama' they say. OK. What is? Well – being moved, getting to the core of a character, that's drama. Certainly not 'polemic' or worse still political opinions: they are boring. Even though, as I think it's our poet who writes: The Mitchell Theatre may be 'full up, enthusiastic' – he however, 'feels like the spectre at the feast. Quite unrepentant however.' One certainty is that it is no help to be Scottish. In the same piece our poet writes of *The Albannach*, a novel he has not actually read – nor does he intend to: 'Novels of this kind are apprentice work in world terms, and you only have to compare them with *real* "Portraits of the Artist" to see how second-rate our culture is.' The news that Scots culture is 'second-rate' will come as a surprise to many, but is the premise upon which both Professor Jan MacDonald and her Committee base their criteria, and their plans for the future.

They also indicate that popularity is not a criterion: one assessor writes: 'Pretty well full of course – easily the most depressing feature of the whole experience.' Obviously the definition of being 'moved', seen above to be a sure sign of drama, does not extend to being moved by 'information'. If I may quote again: 'I do wish they'd take on board the fact that the average member of the audience is not likely to be deeply affected on hearing a list of nineteenth-century grannies beaten over the head by the villainous agents of oppression.' As another assessement says: 'Her story should have angered, and moved and inspired. Instead I came away with none of these emotions – I simply felt informed.' So information, polemic, political stance, and any of this second-rate Scottish stuff is out. Some form of social realist or naturalist dramaturgy is vaguely acceptable. Brecht has never existed, Joan Littlewood and Clifford Odets should never have bothered – 'any theatrical style other than that of emotional, psychologised bourgeois naturalism is some unprecedented experiment.' Such is the level of criticism, the 'standards of excellence' aspired to by Mogg's Arts Council in Scotland.

In this, they may well be a few years behind their counterparts in England. But they'll catch up with Tom Stoppard very soon, in an incoherent sort of way, and the confusion will be all the greater.

Rather than dwelling any longer on this valueless assortment of prejudice, let us turn briefly to Croce: 'It seems' – he writes, in *Culture and Moral Life*, published in 1922 of all times – 'we all agree in wanting an art which resembles that of the Risorgimento and not, for example, the period of D'Annunzio. Actually, however, if one thinks about it, this desire does not imply a preference for one kind of art over another but for a certain moral reality over another'.

And that is indeed what the extraordinary incoherence about the content of this artistic 'excellence' all adds up to: a preference for a certain kind of moral reality.

Perhaps some inkling of the preferred moral reality can be seen in two interesting publications – *Corporate Beanos*, and *A New Way to Enjoy the Theatre*:

*Corporate Beanos*:
Tickets for a West End play, a day at the races, strawberries and cream at Wimbledon, clay-pigeon shooting weekends, wine tastings, trips to exotic overseas locations – the scope of corporate entertainment offerings is huge already – and growing all the time as more and more companies come to appreciate its value in fostering good relations with staff or customers and others see opportunities of taking their slice of the action by entering the business of providing corporate entertainment programmes.

Wine shipper Grants of St James, for instance, have recently started a subsidiary offering a corporate entertainment package which comprises a visit to a country house hotel where wine tastings are hosted by experts in the field.

London-based Corporate Events is among the companies which started off providing hard-to-get tickets for such events as the Cup Final, Henley, Wimbledon and the theatre, expanded into organising the corporate entertainment required at such events and has now gone into the third level of the business by actually creating its own events, tailor-made to customers' requirements.

As their Charles Gay put it: 'Corporate entertainment fulfills a number of purposes; as encouragement and recognition for those who have put their back into a company's success; as hospitality for loyal clients; for those times when you want to tell the outside world about the company, its products and activities, and as a good way to get results from the media.'

And here is 'A New Way to Enjoy the Theatre, exclusively for Gold Cardmembers . . . There's never been a better time to visit London's theatreland.' It advises:

*Les Misérables, – Me and My Girl – 42nd Street – Follies* – with shows of so much richness and diversity, London in 1988 is indisputably the world capital of theatre.

When you book either the Grosvenor House or the Westbury (on the Gold Card, of course) you also ask them to book your tickets for one of these rich, diverse shows. Then your pleasure begins:

The Grosvenor House has created Night Owls and Early Birds to allow you to see the show, and enjoy an excellent and unhurried meal, paced throughout the evening.

The evening begins from 6pm with champagne, followed by your first course. You are then chauffeur-driven to the theatre of your choice. In the interval, you'll find a half bottle of champagne waiting for you, on ice, in the theatre bar.

After the performance, you are chauffeur-driven back

to Grosvenor House – to enjoy your main course and dessert.

This service is available at an extra charge of £35 per person for a group of four or more, and at £42 per person for a group of less than four.

There are, of course, more serious works on offer at the great emporia of high culture: there is more to the programme of the new National Theatre than *Guys and Dolls*, more good work in The Pit and The Swan than *The Glums*, but there are strong connections. The National and the RSC are the very Everests of excellence – the paradigms for the 'new centres of excellence' which follow their lead with much more of the same. These exclusive culinary experiences for Gold Card members are not a million miles from the kind of moral reality of our enterprise culture. But they are a million miles from the experience and the values of most working, or unemployed people. When I read that it made me think of an occasion last October, when we decided to take *Mairi Mhor* to Eriskay. You get there from Barra or South Uist: we took the tiny ferry from Eoligarry on Barra. It was a stormy day, and a high tide, and as we stood with our skips and lights and instruments in the lashing rain on the slippery strip of jetty, we had to wait for the boat to come up ten feet on a wave, throw on a skip, wait, throw on the daughter, wait, jump on ourselves – then a bouncy ride over the Sound to a quieter disembarkation. A new hall, but no food, no pub, no landlady – but a shop. The daughter (8) and I bought and cooked a small roast of lamb with two veg, tatties and gravy in the hall kitchen, while the company got set up. It was such a bad night very few came out. We were told they were also deterred by the exorbitant price of the tickets, £4 or £2.50, which they simply could not afford. But it was a great culinary experience, all the same. The next morning as I paid the boatman, I reflected that one person in a group of less than four would have paid more for his Night Owl and Early Bird experience than we took on Eriskay from the whole audience: and the car would have cost four times more from Park Lane to Shaftesbury Avenue than the boat from Barra to Eriskay – and back. Our singer is from Barra, and I had an advance copy of the cassette we produced of her songs, which the boatman loved so much I had to leave it with him to keep him company over the humps and slides of the Eriskay tides.

Yes, we are talking about different values, a war between the entrepreneurs hungry for profit, action and corporate Beanos, and The Resistance, the people barely scraping a living, and having their living and their culture threatened by these people living more than a million miles away. They are Gaelic speakers who love the songs but can't afford £4 to go to a show on their own island. The other lot fly Concorde to Morocco to launch a product, eat their way through 'theme menus', or enjoy the Company Hospitality package for the British Grand Prix, with I quote, 'marquee champagne reception, five-course lunch, complimentary bar, and colour TV', at £1,188 for a table for six.

There can be no simple geographical divisions: there are people without the price of a loaf in London, and there are certainly entrepreneurs in the Western Isles. And there is no monopoly of virtue or high moral standards in the dispossessed or the unemployed. But we are not talking about individual, or geographically defined morality: we are talking about a society – and we live in a society, in spite of Mrs Thatcher's attempts to reduce it to an aggregate of competing individuals. The morality of a society is expressed in political decisions: its values are the responsibility of all its members.

To come back to the 7:84 (Scotland) saga. I don't wish to use these inept assessments of our work, and the theatrical and moral values they represent as an excuse for our failings as a company. We clearly have had many, particularly over the last few years, and along with other companies have felt the financial squeeze, and tussled with many difficulties. But if provision of theatre to every part of Scotland was a criterion, we certainly met it; and if the judgement of Sorley MacLean is to be trusted, the performance of *Mairi Mhor* was excellent: a different kind of excellence from Mogg's but excellent.

I would not like you to think 7:84 was cut because of these criticisms, however. As I see it, these – and the criticisms of the administration and the Board – were not reasons but justifications for a cut. A year or so ago, the then chairman of the SAC was a damp-ish Tory. He was managing director of a large firm. His proprietor was Scottish Chairman, and is now UK Chairman of the Economic League – a right-wing bosses' organisa-tion that keeps a ludicrous black-list of undesirables who should not be employed. As I said earlier, it was revealed that my name was prominent on a list leaked from its North-West of England files. Even so, when asked whether 7:84 (Scotland) would be axed like 7:84 (England), he indicated that he would resist similar political repression in Scotland. Strange, given his boss's connection with the Economic League. But that is what he said.

He was replaced last year by Professor Sir Alan Peacock, one of Thatcher's trusted academics, who had just produced a report for her on the future of the BBC. Within months, 7:84 was cut. Sir Alan says to suggest that 7:84 was cut for political reasons is 'evil nonsense'. Is it?

*          *          *

However, the world is a wide and wonderful place, and there are joys and encouragement all over it.

During this last year or two, we have been very fortunate in meeting a lot of people from other parts of the world working in our area of theatre, and seeing what they do. Many come to Mayfest, the Glasgow festival of popular theatre and music; others we have met on tours to other countries, at festivals in Berlin, Toronto, Cape Breton, Adelaide, Wellington, Avignon, and even Edinburgh. It is of the greatest value to us to realise how far our kind of work has spread, and how much support we can give one another. The war between the dispossessed, the voiceless, the powerless, the victims of the scramble to the top, and the institutions set up to exploit them, police them, culturally diminish them, keep them in their place, is world-wide – and increasingly theatre is playing a crucial part in what Augusto Boal calls 'empowering' people: giving them a voice, solidarity with one another, an identity and a hope for the future.

Quite apart from the groups still left in Britain (which includes Wildcat, Borderline, Monstrous Regiment, Welfare State, and many local and young people's theatre companies), the world is full of exciting theatre-makers and companies. Nearly all have some form of collective structure, and the general aims outlined above. They have different roles in different societies of course.

In the emerging countries they are helping to define their popular culture or to redefine it for the end of the twentieth century, helping to radicalise or criticise elements of it, or to define the aims of their societies. Sistren, for example, an outrageously entertaining company from Jamaica, is an all-woman collective telling stories with music in a highly popular idiom, but fighting against male aggression, fighting to make a new generation of Jamaican men conscious of the way their fathers treat, and see, women. Jagran, from India, is a large group of very poor children from the streets who have learnt amazing skills with masks and tumbling, including a disabled boy, with no legs, on a trolley; their great contribution must be to show what people can do if they work together. In Zimbabwe, and I believe other countries in Africa, there are companies grappling with the huge social problems of urbanisation, and industrialisation, and what that is doing to the traditional culture. After Allende came to power in Chile, groups of theatre-workers went to live in small communities, rural or urban, and began to create theatre under the instruction of the people around them: dramatising events of significance, showing the people who were making their lives miserable, celebrating their victories. To a smaller extent this still goes on, in very difficult circumstances, in Chile today, organised by Chileans who became friends while in exile here, who have with great courage gone back to do this work. They may be tortured again, even disappear and die for it.

In Cuba the theatre, dance and music movements have certainly helped re-define a national culture, and bring great joyfulness to the lives of everybody, wherever they live. In those Third World countries that are fighting for or have won a popular socialist government, the role of theatre in giving definition to the new morality cannot be overestimated.

We met a great group from Nicaragua, named Teo-Coyanni. They were invited to Mayfest, then we really got to know them in Cape Breton, Nova Scotia and later in Montreal. The oldest was no more than 22, several 15 or 16. They play in the war-zone of Nicaragua, where the Contras are killing people and sabotaging the reconstruction of the countryside. They always have to carry guns, and some go for military service from time to time. As they arrive in a village, they spend the morning demonstrating new agricultural techniques, informing the campesinos of developments in seeds and fertiliser, drainage and livestock. In the evening they give their show. Mogg would think it had to be solemn, sloganising, boring, non-theatrical polemics. Well, the show I saw certainly has revolutionary content, in one way, being a re-enactment of early pre-Christian myth, but it was full of music, poetry, imagery, masks, huge elaborate ritual artefacts, and a great sense of fun. It would have livened up an evening in the war-zone very satisfactorily, but as far as form went it had more in common with WB Yeats than the Salford Red Megaphones. They did not take the women members of the company into their more dangerous areas, because the Contras reserved their most hideous practices for captured women. Reagan, and now Bush, pay these Contras. Our Mrs Thatcher rushes off to Washington to greet Bush, offer us as his Number One Ally. Nicaragua is closer than we think. The links between us and Teo-Coyanni are not just sentimental.

Many companies in the more industrialised countries are in the business of asserting the presence of certain dispossessed groups – whether oppressed by class, gender or race. The women's groups that now exist all over Canada are a good example. We met many of them. They had moved on from humourless complaining to exploring the rich seam of farce, comedy, tragedy and idiocy at the interface between women and men. Syrens, Hysterical Women, Arlene Mantle, the women in the Catalyst group, the native Indian women who came to Edinburgh with a very violent play about violence to women, the women in some of Passe Murailles's productions, the Women's Theatre Space in Montreal are part of a large, growing theatre movement to give voice to the lives of women in Canada. From Australia there are many more, some very strong, some strident, all highly active.

As for assertions of class, and building the cultural and political self-confidence of the working class or a peasant class, we have come across too many to spell out. In the US, the New York Labor Theatre, Bread and Roses in Chicago, the San Francisco Mime Troupe, and in the Hispanic worker communities along the West Coast the Teatro Campesino, are all making – or all made, since some no longer exist – at least some impact on the lives of the great American working class, have tried to make it aware of its own problems, and of its responsibilities in the world.

In Australia Sidetracks in Sydney, Junction Theatre in Adelaide, and many more, work hard. I saw Sidetracks in a suburban Town Hall in South Australia perform a new piece about the new forms of colonial oppression, directed beautifully by Don Mamouney, that was one of the best pieces of theatre I have seen in Australia. More recently I saw a piece about ethnic tensions between immigrants in a school – performed in a school – which was a bit schematic and lacked any fire, but was very much to the point, and enjoyed by the largely school-going audience. Junction is very small, working on very local issues from a disused church in Adelaide – Malcolm Blaylock and his team are thoroughly integrated into the traditionally strong radical culture of the workers of that area. They research single issues with larger implications, and entertain and encourage their audiences with some funny, musical and direct work. Standing outside one of their waterside gigs, looking out towards the Antarctic, I began to feel that this kind of theatre work really had gone round the world; staying with Malcolm, I also realised that we were not alone – we had friends, comrades, whose solidarity is a tremendous source of strength.

Another group with whom we found real friendship and fellow-feeling was Le Theatre Parminou, based in Victoriaville in Quebec. These Quebecois who perform in French and sometimes English bring a wonderfully eccentric imagination to their work – which in itself is usually very targeted thematically. One show we saw was about pornography and how it works, who sells it, who buys it etc. They created a gallery of large-dimension characters, used very effective theatre techniques, were wonderful comic and tragic actors, and were hugely entertaining. They have worked together for many years, and have a very impressive, mature way of relating within the company, and have remained very much a group, but also very, very individual: something we have to learn about in this country.

I would love to talk a lot more about the way the other groups we know work and live – the Werktheater in Holland, the 20 or 30 companies in the Canadian Theatre Alliance, the 60 or 70 companies in Sweden, the people trying to work this way in New Zealand, with great support from the New Zealand TUC. I would love to go into detail over the companies from South Africa, mostly under the umbrella of the Market

Theatre, Johannesburg – productions like *Woza Albert, Poppie Nangena*, and hundreds of others – thrilling, expressive, informative theatre, a part of their history.

But there are too many. Suffice it to say these companies are a new force in the western world, giving voice to an international alternative 'moral reality'.

I will, however, point to another role of this kind of theatre: the defence of a people, drawing attention on a large scale to the destruction of a culture, a way of life. Jack Davies's plays about the aborigine people in Australia have done more to alert people there, and here, to the damage inflicted on them than any government, and are pressurising the government to do something. My friend David Diamond from Headlines in Vancouver has just created a play with a tribe of Inuit people in the north of British Columbia which is forming the spearhead of their fight to get their tribal lands restored to them. It explores not only the illegality of the white settlement, but sets out to show the huge cultural feeling for the land, and the complex differences between their relationship with land and that of the white settlers which reveals so much else of a deep and complex nature about them as groups of people. The show turns defence into attack, conservation into celebration, legality into lived experience. Another show, this time from Labrador on the Atlantic coast of Canada, explores the effect of militarisation and enforced settlement in shanty-towns of the native people there, and has involved them in acting out their dramas in a way that is both clarifying for them and illuminating for us.

Of the 'alternative' theatres that have played the biggest part in my theatrical thinking, it is the big, celebratory companies that loom largest. The work of the smaller companies like Parminou and Het Werktheater in

Holland is of course very close to ours, and has meant a great deal over the years, but on looking around now for a way to combat the apathy, defeatism, sense of guilt and failure, sheer exhaustion of the alternative theatre in Britain, I look to four great companies – Ariane Mnouchkine's Théâtre du Soleil, Jerome Savary's Grand Magic Circus, Ronconi's Teatro Libero di Roma in the late 60s, and Circus Oz.

I will, I hope, come next week to a consideration of ways forward, and positives for the future.

For the present, I will just finish by trying to sum up the values and roles of alternative theatre – as I've encountered it. Firstly it can contribute to a definition, a revaluation of the cultural identity of a people or a section of society, can add to the richness and diversity of that identity. Secondly, it can assert, draw attention to, give voice to threatened communities, can, by allowing them to speak, help them to survive. Thirdly, it can mount an attack on the standarisation of culture and consciousness which is a function of late industrial/early technological 'consumerist' societies everywhere. Fourthly, it can be and often is linked to a wider political struggle for the right of a people or a section of a society to control its own destiny, to 'self-determination'. Fifthly, it can make a challenge to the values imposed on it from a dominant group – it can help to stop ruling class, or ruling race, or male, or multi-national capitalist values being 'universalised' as common sense, or self-evident truth: as such, it presents a challenge also to the state's cultural engineers, in Ministries of Culture, Arts Councils, universities, schools and the media.

These alternative theatres, of which more objective, complete and properly researched histories are now being written, on the whole embody Croce's 'different moral realities'. As such, they will constantly come under attack, and threat of annihilation, from the dominant 'moral reality', and, as Croce observed, this attack will frequently be disguised as 'artistic preference'. But the worldwide growth in practically every capitalist country, and many socialist ones, is ensuring that it will not be wiped out so easily. We do not seek to wipe out bourgeois cultures. We do not exclude high culture from people's lives. One of the bases of this work is the flowering of many thousand blossoms – of culture, theatre, form, and moral reality – that should never be bitten by the frost of autocracy, of bigotry in powerful places, or of incompetent, lazy thinking.

# 6

# Celebration, Spectacle, Carnival

In the last few talks I have been trying to describe the processes of cultural change over the last ten years, and to personalise it by describing my experiences of the attempts to cut, marginalise or destroy the work of 7:84 Theatre Company. We have looked at key changes in the areas of class-consciousness, the uses of the state, the idea of the nation, and the danger of cultural standardisation in a post-industrial mass-media-dominated Britain. Last week we began to look outside the British Isles to the simultaneous flowering of popular theatre in many other countries, and of the hope this gives that this particular genre will survive the temporary setback it is undoubtedly suffering under a profit-maximising government.

I should like in this last talk to look at four of the companies whose work I particularly admire and find fruitful, and look at ways forward, ways to create new forms of popular theatre that may celebrate human and social values other than business efficiency and strong lager.

But first a look at those values, the life-experience of the money-oriented society we live in.

It has to be said that the resources of the human imagination are endless, that even in the most extreme of deprived conditions, human beings will find some richness of the mind, some fertility of the fantasy. This, however, is no vindication of deprivation. A brief look at the government's recent (1989) White Paper on Television and Radio will show very painfully that we are in the hands of people with no concern for cultural well-being. Their reassurances about the nature of broadcasting rely on people in the media continuing to fight against them, to try to defend a set of values which they do everything to discourage.

This may well not happen for much longer. There will always be people wanting to make TV programmes as long as it pays well, but the quality of their ideas depends greatly on what is being looked for, and on the chances of the idea being properly executed. Both of these depend on the taste and the priorities of the executives in charge of a station. If the executives are appointed solely for their ability to get programmes on the air cheaply and bring in the biggest possible audience, which is clearly what all the new structures demand, then British television will become the cultural equivalent of junk-food – without nourishment or pleasure, spiced by cheap chemical additives, and available at all hours.

Of course some people will think it worth struggling to stem the tide of polluted waste, and of course they may occasionally succeed, which alas will then be used to prove how wonderful the new ways of the market-force really are. And I have no doubt the White Paper is going to become enshrined in a Broadcasting Act that will bring these values to television.

But it will, of course, be strictly controlled in its dealings with life below the waist, and will never be allowed to offend public decency or outrage the suburbs of Guildford, thanks to Poo Bah Mogg, who is now in charge of the new Broadcasting Standards Council. It is entirely consistent with this philosophy that 'standards' are seen as essentially negative, censorious and prudish things. These 'standards' are expressions of the pinched paranoia of the same narrow band of English bourgeois moralists as the ill-defined concept of 'excellence' that is playing such a destructive role in the Arts Council's new order: Mrs Whitehouse transmogrified. For the role of the British Standards Council is to enforce puritanical moral values onto a mass of television which will be otherwise totally *un*regulated. Social, artistic, representational responsibilities are thrown to the winds: but 'bad' language and sexual behaviour will be expensively and ruthlessly policed. By Lord Mogg in person.

I dwell on television's perils first because the new proposals for it are a perfect statement of the cultural values of our society, and it is of course the most important cultural nexus in our society. If we look a little more closely at the content of these shows which the new breed of executive thinks will justify launching a satellite in orbit around the earth to transmit, then the contradictions and the cultural confusions of our society become apparent.

Firstly, of course, television sells America, hour by hour, day by day, year by year. An America full of murderers, crooked cops, nasty oil tycoons, fabulously rich and charming people, and power: the power to dominate the world. And we have grown to love it, this America. Our own programmes try to imitate its slick dialogue, its cynical cleverness, its violence, its intrigues, and its obsession with money and power, leading to fame, respect and adulation. These values come from our own society now, as well as American television. They have reinforced each other.

Secondly, the new TV sells sport: competition of all kinds, as cruel, as dangerous, as ruthless as possible. Indoor bowls can become a paradigm of skilful, poker-faced deal-making, the opponent's bowl being 'taken out' at the last minute to crush the opposition. Even in snooker, the deadly cool, dead-eyed and efficient, silent activity of a Steve Davies commands our applause, not least for the cut-aways to the defeated ruefulness of the opponent on the seat, in whose impotence we glory. This may sound fanciful, but a comparison between the emotions roused by *Dallas*, a Grand Prix car race, and the attempts by Guinness to take over Distillers as portrayed on the news nightly, would I think produce some interestingly similar patterns. The old sports; soccer, cricket, rugby, will surely become less important on television as Sumo wrestling and Australian-rules football capture the teenage imagination. Horse-racing is an ideal sport, combining competition, danger and loadsamoney, but is expensive to cover. Perhaps Scalectric car-racing with bookies and odds on racers will replace it, as it is easy to do in the studio.

Thirdly, the new television sells sentiment and nostalgia. The range of emotions that its executives ascribe to the mass viewer is very narrow. The 'Ooh!' of the boxing-ring, The 'Aah!' of the nostalgic drama, and the 'Oh dear!' of the soap opera, seems to be about it, or will be when all programmes are aimed at a worldwide mass audience. The real world does percolate into this miasma of the feebler emotions, but only gently and on a certain level – AIDS, ecological problems, unemployment do exist, but are transmuted into occasions for sadness, regret, or stoic acceptance. Resistance is seen as political,

ergo comic – usually given to a callow youth who doesn't
understand. The past is always better, associated with
more orderly times, people being nice to each other,
Britain being dignified, and lovely costumes.

Fourthly, the new television ascribes to women a role
in society which accords perfectly with Thatcherite moral
views on the woman's duty to be at home, breeding and
keeping out of the unemployment figures. The woman is
the receptacle for the male fantasy of the folk-memory –
for gardening skills, cookery, child care, house-care, in
the first instance, but also for love for and knowledge
of wild life, animals, the countryside, old people, and a
large sector of the fictional past. There are efforts to carry
more active, grown-up images of women, by giving them
male attributes and guns, but this is largely fantasy-land:
their real job is to be full of all the warm, magical, old love
and skills that the executive is too busy to acquire, and
with them to enhance his spare time. Women continue
to be seen as sex-objects, to be used for desire, status
or aggression purposes. But in programming terms, it is
the image of woman as fecund with domestic skills that
dominates, especially during the day. Television seems
unaware of this, merely seeing the opportunity for a
captive audience who accept the definitions ascribed
to them. A TV executive said to me recently: 'Our
audience is mostly old, poor and women!' The way he
said women made it clear that they were a group he
regretted having to make programmes for. The new
channels will, I think, compound this use of the image of
women in order to sell products women buy.

Television sells news as a commodity, as a set of tricks
or disasters adding up to a fictional construct of the world
seen in terms of the newsworthy. Increasingly this narrative will unfold as gobbets of unexplored sensationalism,

as saleable tit-bits of spiced-up information, rather than genuinely informative reporting of events. As the new satellites and micro-waves and city stations and Channel 5 come in, today's commercial radio news will sound like Gibbons' *Decline and Fall*. The values built in to the news already are profoundly conservative – they will become more like *The Sun* the more the Rupert Murdochs of this world own them.

And television is advertising. Even greater numbers of commercials, with ever diminishing control over what goes into them, the life-values they promote, the insidious techniques they use to sell their product. Commercials sell consumerism, envy, greed, debased images of women, trivialised images of children, superficiality and the inability to choose rationally or to concentrate for longer than twenty-five seconds. I believe they do not, on balance, make a positive contribution to society.

In its way, even so, television represents many of the positive aspects of our culture at the moment. These Cassandra-like warnings are, I'm sure, justified by the evidence of the model the new order chooses to praise: American television, of course, with its wonderful multiplicity of choice! This image of television, the dominant form of popular culture, and of television's future is of course already with us, co-existing with the positive and the valuable. Our television already is US-dominated, full of competitive sport, sentiment, nostalgia, and degrading images of women. Its values *are* consumerist, repressive and conservative. But at the moment it has people within it working against these values, these images of our world. Many of them are working against it in an élitist or excluding way, and do what they can – others take it on as a popular medium. What is important is that with the new set-up, there will be fewer and fewer of these people, and less incentive for them to fight.

But popular taste is moving, or being steered, towards the snappy, the violent, the spuriously exciting, the macabre, the gladiatorial, the cosy. In this way television is both cause and result of shifts in popular culture, and a useful weather forecast for future troughs moving across the Atlantic.

But it does manage to carry within it traces of a popular culture long suppressed – the Saturnalian liberties of Spitting Image, the broad panto of some of Morecambe and Wise, the Grimaldi of Frankie Howerd, the deep interest in nature's freaks and monsters, as well as a care for the natural world, in some wild-life programmes, and the simple curiosity about the neighbours as seen in the best of the *40 Minutes* series and other good documentaries.

What is missing is life, size, contact with others in an audience, community. Communal celebration of events, stories, songs is not possible. The whole dimension is going not only from the television, but from our whole lives. Most *live* mass popular culture now is a spin-off from or an imitation of television or radio – pantos, pop-concerts, West End musicals all are inspired by and aspire to the nature of TV light entertainment. And as the positive elements of television get more difficult to achieve, and the New Order values become more enshrined in TV and the same forces that brought this about are brought to bear upon the popular culture, so that culture will become, in its mass form, ever more in need of challenge, of contestation from other views of the world and society.

What then is there with the force and range and roots in the popular which can even begin to take on such a job?

First of all it has to be said that to challenge this apparently inexorable, self-propelling, self-propagating force on its own ground and on its own terms is a most difficult project, and one that has led many to despair. Nevertheless there are contradictions within all the structures of cultural power, and people who can see the necessity to encourage or at least allow alternative voices. The availability of *more* channels on TV, for example, *may* allow a greater variety of programme – but will certainly debase the impact of any one programme. The overall social force of TV, however, will not be improved by the changes to come.

But the other route is *not* to take on this dominant popular culture on its own ground, but to shift, to open up new – or perhaps old – areas of the culture so successfully excluded from all that I have been sketching in. The image of a human being allowed by the telly-culture is so narrow, so minimal, so strait-jacketed that it is indeed not difficult to move fruitfully outside it, and into a whole world of human possibilities.

It was with some joy, for example, that I read this passage:

Laughter in the Middle Ages remained outside all official spheres of ideology and outside strict forms of social relations. Laughter was eliminated from religious cult, from feudal and state ceremonials, etiquette, and from all the genres of high speculation. An intolerant, one-sided tone of seriousness is characteristic of official medieval culture. The very contents of medieval ideology – asceticism, sombre providentialism, pain, atonement, suffering, as well as the character of the feudal regime, with its oppression and intimidation – all these elements determined this tone of icy petrified seriousness. It was supposedly the only tone fit to express the true, the good, and all that was essential and meaningful. Fear, religious awe, humility, these were the overtones of this seriousness.

Early Christianity had already condemned laughter. Tertullian, Cyprian, and John Chrysostom preached against ancient spectacles, especially against the mime and the mime's jests and laughter. John Chrysostom declared that jests and laughter are not from God but from the devil. Only permanent seriousness, remorse, and sorrow for his sins befit the Christian. During the struggle against the Aryans, Christians were accused of introducing elements of the mime – song, gesticulation, laughter – into religious services.

But this intolerant seriousness of the official church ideology made it necessary to legalize the gaiety, laughter and jests which had been eliminated from the canonized ritual and etiquette. Thus forms of pure laughter were created parallel to the official forms.

At the same time certain religious cults inherited from antiquity were influenced by the East and in some cases by local pagan rites, especially by the rites of fertility. Rudiments of gaiety and laughter are present in these forms. They can be found in the liturgy and in funeral rites, as well as in the rites of baptism, of marriage and in other religious services. But these rudiments are sublimated and toned down. If performed in a zone near a church, they had to be authorized. These rites of pure laughter were even permitted as a parallel to the official cults.

Such were, first of all, the 'feast of fools' (*festa stultorum, fatuorum, follorum*) which were celebrated by schoolmen and lower clerics on the feast of St Stephen, on New Year's Day, on the feast of the Holy Innocents, of the Epiphany, and of St John. These celebrations were originally held in the churches and bore a fully legitimate character. Later they became only semi-legal, and at the end of the Middle Ages were completely banned from the churches but continued to exist in the streets and in taverns, where they were absorbed into carnival merriment and amusements. The 'feast of fools' showed a particular obstinacy and force of survival in France (*fête des fous*). This feast was actually a parody and travesty of the official cult, with masquerades and improper dances. These celebrations, held by the lower clergy, were especially boisterous on New Year's Day and on Epiphany.

Nearly all the rituals of the 'feast of fools' are a grotesque degradation of various church rituals and symbols and their transfer to the material bodily level: gluttony and drunken orgies on the altar table, indecent gestures, disrobing.

It was precisely the one-sided character of official seriousness which led to the necessity of creating a vent for the second nature of man, for laughter. The 'feast of fools', at least once a year, became a vent for laughter; the material bodily principle linked with it then enjoyed complete freedom. Here we have an unambiguous recognition of the second festive life of medieval man.

Laughter at the 'feast of fools' was not, of course, an abstract and purely negative mockery of the Christian ritual and the Church's hierarchy. The negative derisive element was deeply immersed in the triumphant theme of bodily regeneration and renewal. It was 'man's second nature' that was laughing, the lower bodily stratum which could not express itself in official cult and ideology.

The concept of an unofficial, Rabelaisian merry-making which is licensed to mock, parody and create obscene versions of the official, solemn, censorious world of church and state, is one that might well have had a meaning in Stalin's Russia, when Bakhtin the Soviet critic wrote that; and it certainly has a meaning in Thatcher's Britain.

The idea of 'carnival', as expressed by Bakhtin, again may need qualification in terms of history, and of its attitudes to women, but remains very attractive in the twentieth century. His idea of carnival expressing the 'whole' human being, eating, drinking, defecating and copulating, as well as thinking, praying and wielding power, obscene as well as divine, is something that has meaning when set against the narrowness of the concept of humanity in mass telly-culture. And it is to this general area of celebratory, public, all-inclusive theatre that maybe we should turn when we think of contesting, rather than trying to produce theatre that is political in the same way that bourgeois theatre is; instead of saying different things with the same squeaky voice, perhaps we ought to be looking for a whole new vocal range.

Of course we would certainly be courting disaster to assume a medieval sensibility lurking within a modern audience. I would prefer to read Bakhtin's visions of carnival, laughter and 'wholeness' as inspirational rather than either historical accounts or as a model to imitate.

Having said that, I would like to point to an odd kind of congruity. With the Education Act of 1944, whole generations of children of working-class families were exposed to the legitimate theatre – as to many other areas of life – for the very first time. Many so exposed made massive contributions to it, finding ways to enrich and expand legitimate theatre with their new range of experience, feeling and ways of seeing.

Due to the hierarchy of genres, legit theatre was chosen as their form, rather than any new or even old form. They were persuaded by the culture machine that it was the highest form of dramatic expression, especially if it was in London, above all at the Royal Court. An intelligent and tradition-conscious writer like John Arden, in his early plays, was bringing fragments of an older popular tradition into the framework of bourgeois plays – the ballads of *Musgrave*, the songs and the language of *Live*

*Like Pigs*, were fitted into a bourgeois theatre form, and presented to a (very small) audience of cosmopolitan culture-purveyors. But as time went by, Arden – now working with D'Arcy – began to turn over the form as well: *The Ballygombeen Bequest* being the finest example, though their 'Muggins' play with CAST, and I believe some of their street theatre, broke the formal barriers as well.

What possibly was happening, as we found our feet and our voice in theatre, was that we began to liberate into dramatic shape not only our experience, the content of the work, but also our feeling for the form of theatre, inherited, resuscitated or generated afresh from the feeling for theatre, and its forms, of the working classes. This may be a fanciful generalisation, but it certainly means something to me. What is intriguing at this point in history is the question: 'Have we gone far enough?' Given the horrific appropriation of popular culture, the 'Poisoning of the Water' that we have seen over the last decade, do those of us who are fighting for a popular culture that has socialist values not need to go a lot further away from the legitimate theatre in every way? Should we be making oppositional statements in the same measured, if squeaky voice, or should we be reinventing, rediscovering theatre with a glorious five-octave range? Obviously, I think we should be trying to achieve the latter.

To return to my practice in 7:84, I would say that we tried to create new forms, extend the range, break the barriers, etc. But over the last five years in Scotland the pressure was strongly and steadily towards moving the work back into an 'oppositional' but legitimate form. These pressures, the administrative preoccupations, the involvement of television in our work, and the fight to save 7:84 (England), against right and zombie left, all conspired, in a hardening policital climate, to put me as a writer/theatre-maker on the defensive. It took the Arts Council's final impertinent list of demands that I should betray not only my friends, and the guiding principles of the company, but also the formal recklessness that was one of the main creative urges behind the company, that made me first of all break with the Arts Council by refusing to comply, and then ask with much greater urgency the questions about form, and range, that I ask here.

The real answers, naturally, will be in the work that emerges. Whether that connects with a popular audience in a fruitful way is the only criterion of success, for me at least. Others may, and I hope will, go further and do better.

So in the context of the commercialised immiseration of mass popular culture, the concept of a new carnival theatre, and my own personal needs to move forward, I'd like to turn briefly to the four companies I mentioned last week as having a particular significance: Ronconi's Teatro Libero, Ariane Mnouchkine's Théâtre du Soleil, Jerome Savary's Grand Magic Circus and Circus Oz.

On the face of it Savary's great circus-cum-cabaret-cum-anarchist event is nearer to the model of liberating pageant than the others. Savary first came to London with an outrageous production of an Arrabal surreal piece, heavily influenced by Jarry, with lavatorial events, bare-bollock young actors flying or swinging out over the audience, cruelty of various kinds, some very beautiful young men and women, and a dreamlike discontinuity to it all: shards of nightmare and erotica collected into a challenging bundle. Savary came back with his Grand Magic Circus, another collection of dreams, music, erotica and drama, playing to large audiences in the Roundhouse. He came back to London with a show about, it said, Chairman Mao, of a similar kind. He went on to run a large theatre on the smart side of the Seine, and to make many productions. Now he has taken over one of the regional Centres of Culture.

The problem with Jerome's dramaturgy is, or was, his misplaced sense of pride. He absolutely insisted that theatre, especially popular theatre, should not be subsidised. In argument, he claimed that subsidy made it 'art', not truly popular, therefore not good. We contended that this was rubbish, but as he was playing to large popular audiences all over Europe, he was at that time, 1972, in a strong position. I am convinced this rather macho desire for self-sufficiency was his undoing, as he was forced into more and more slick showmanship, more pandering to the whimsicality of the audience, less to the alliance of surrealism and carnival that was his strength, but which was a more vulnerable style and needed protection, artistic and financial, from the self-imposed pressures of the market-place.

Ronconi, an Italian director, was not afraid of subsidy, but other pressures have taken him far away from his early production style which was, for me, a seminal experience. His production for Teatro Libero di Roma of a version of Ariosto's *Orlando Furioso* came to the Haymarket Ice Rink in Edinburgh in, I think, 1969. It was a production designed for Italian piazzas, notably those of the Tuscan towns, to be performed during festivals. The action happened on free-wheeling platforms zooming around among the audience, with sometimes three or four stories at one time being acted out or declaimed in various parts of the space. It was a very energetic performance, requiring a lot from the audience, but getting it because of the appealing boldness of the actors and the sense it all generated of too much too fast, but very exciting. There was a great feeling of pageantry and, when the *coup de théâtre* of the appearance of the Hippogriffe happened, of amazing spectacle. It relates to the carnival idea, at least to the spectacular element of carnival, and again was very popular in Italy and elsewhere. Ronconi went on to explore staging more in experimental theatre than in popular theatre, and trivialised the fruits of his early work.

Ariane Mnouchkine's theatre is hardly a workers' theatre, though she has a wide following from all classes in Paris and elsewhere. Its great achievement is in its use of space and movement, design and staging, allied with splendidly sensitive yet physical performance. The company's transformations of their ammunition factory, the Cartoucherie in the Bois de Vincennes, are spectacular. Their first production there was *1789*, the story told in an oppositional-historical way, of the first years of the French Revolution. Mnouchkine's text is ironic, comic, and savage in turns. In a way it celebrates the Fiesta of those years, the coming alive of the streets of Paris, the *Chahut* or rucking of the people, the hysterical comedy and ridiculous tragedies of the public events of the time. When I saw it, in 1971 at the Roundhouse, it was the staging that turned it into a carnival event. Taking from medieval theatre the notion of several stages all around the audience, it created a world of action within which the spectator moved and participated by movement; the gathering of the audience around the stage where the scene was taking place became part of the event taking place, the audience were in the play.

Her subsequent productions have explored many different ways of staging, including transforming the whole playing area into a landscape with people living in it for *L'Age d'Or*. The Shakespeare productions using a combination of Samurai costume and movement, and gentle, intimate scenes of great stillness brought a whole new feeling to *Henry IV*, and a multi-sexual libidinousness to *Twelfth Night* which brought out a great deal of the unofficial world in the official play. Since then her *Sihanouk* about Cambodia and her *L'Indiade* about India at the times of the British withdrawal were powerful pieces of theatre perhaps not relevant to the notion of carnival, but rich with ideas it could build on. It is Mnouchkine's *1789* that means most still, and we can all learn a great deal from it.

Of the fourth of my troupes, Circus Oz, all that needs to be said is that here a group of entertainers have worked with total dedication to acquire the popular skills of circus. Based outside Melbourne, they nearly all went to a Chinese circus and acrobatic school, came back and worked together to make a series of shows based on circus, with their own Big Top, that became much more coherent and made more practical statements about Australian society, the human body, gender, sensuality, sexuality and comedy high and low than normal circus rises to. It is their combination of physical skills, bodily splendour and very modern and sharp intelligence that is a pointer to the way popular forms in this country could move forward: not necessarily into circus, but these attributes are necessary for most good popular entertainment, and not in overwhelming supply at the moment. Add to this a sense of the surreal and an eccentric imagination, and Circus Oz has a lot to offer.

From all of these companies came the genuine reek of popular celebration, the daring mix of tragic and comic, the ethereal and the fleshly, the head, the belly and the womb, poetry, obscenity and fecundity that perhaps went some of the way towards a viable contemporary version of Bakhtin's vision of the carnival. It is present also in some of Joan Littlewood's work, notably *The Hostage*, and rears its head from time to time in unexpected corners of plays, in quite a few corners of the great, wonderful and dangerous work of Ken Campbell, especially in his Roadshow days, in some of Welfare State's work, and in some of the new shows coming now from the Soviet Union – like the scene on the roof in *Stars In the Morning Sky*, several scenes in Tumanashvili's Georgian version of *Our Town*, in the clowning in the Moscow State Circus. Undoubtedly it was there in the San Francisco Mime Troupe, in the Campesino Theatre, now and again in Teatro Escambray from Cuba, and certainly in the work of Teo Coyanni from Nicaragua.

Why is this quality important? I think we all know now that a lot will have to change in the world's power-structure before England, or even Scotland, can break out of the capitalist system. Even a Labour government seems far away, let alone a revolution. Things do change, but so much in the basic thinking and feeling habits of the mass of the people has to change before a revolution could be genuinely liberating, even if one came about. There is no point in a revolution that ends up with a new Stalin and new repression. To be worth fighting for, a socialist programme for change must itself find a new vocal range different from the strident roar or the pathetic bleat that are its main sounds today. Socialism needs to re-think its images of humanity, its stereotypes of goodie and baddie, saint and sinner. It needs to find a new vocabulary drawing on this new vision of human possibility, but it must learn this vocabulary from the imagination of the people. So this quality of the popular celebration of humanity in its whole body and extended mind and spirit is, or should be, a preoccupation of all who want to leap beyond the sterile semantics of Westminster, and the despair of conventional political struggle.

If it is allowed by this increasingly authoritarian government, then such a theatre could take its place among the organs of a Resistance Movement that needs to find the popular imagination as well as express post-industrial reality. Of course theatre *alone* cannot, should not and never will achieve a great deal politically; but in the process of trying to articulate a deeply felt complex of thoughts, emotions and desires, and trying to explore and present a greater range of our experiences of living, such a dramatising could bring some new life to our theatre, as well as moving political awareness and giving some self-confidence to some otherwise demoralised or silenced sectors of society – like the working class, those who care about the natural and animal life around us, and those dispossessed of their full potential for living.

The question will be asked: 'Why change what we have? It appears to work, and we as a nation need those goads to private and corporate efficiency to make us competitive with the rest of the world.' Surely we should keep on with our present successes, think positively about them. In the words of Richard Luce, our present Arts Minister:

> You should accept the political and economic climate in which we now live, and make the most of it. Such an attitude of mind could bring surprisingly good results.

Let us assume that we as a society, whether Britain, England, or the South-East of England, hold our present course, maybe for another 12 to 15 years. We will, I think, have created a world populated by a race of efficient, successful monsters, rich, powerful and intolerant, managing a workforce of individualistic, self-seeking sellers of their skills, incapable of solidarity, resenting even paying taxes, also intolerant. Both of these groups – for class will be a non-word – will grow increasingly bitter about 'supporting' the many millions of unemployed, and unemployable people who do not fit in to society's round holes.

Of course all this has been happening for some time. I extrapolate tendencies already there. Ten years ago, even before Thatcher, I was getting off the plane from Edinburgh, at Heathrow. Two old ladies were having difficulty getting their coats on, their bags down from the rack, their bits and pieces into their bags – and holding up the grey ranks of business people trying to get off the plane. The grey people were angry, impatient, suppressing violence, even fury at this display. It suddenly struck me with great force that the two old women were, in terms of our society, 'incompetent'. The idea of competence extends into every area of our lives. It is largely defined negatively, in terms of an individual's or group's failure to *fit into* the mechanised living processes. The airport, with its passenger-handling techniques, is the paradigm of city life. If you are not physically agile, or you are poor, black, too young, old, a woman, imaginative, gay, or militantly disturbing the system, you are deviating from an ideal of competence: you are likely to upset the flow of the machinery, cause hold-ups or disturbances to the annoyance of others, you are a social misfit. The positive definition of the ideal Competent Person is that of an agile enthusiast for the machine, adapting physically, mentally, politically and socially to its demands, able to understand it and accept it, thereby making it work more efficiently. But what is the machine doing? Who is it for? It is partly in the service of the nation-state, in hot competition with others, for survival among the most affluent. Indeed, without generating capital, it becomes less efficient as a machine. Therefore the life-processing machine is there in fact to maintain *itself*. Its benefits to the individual are, of course, mixed. Since it needs health, it will try to help its individuals to be physically healthy. It requires intelligent technologists, and of course economists, so it will encourage education, seek out its functionaries wherever they may be. So schools and hospitals will be bought – and roads. But above all it requires conformity: every individual must be a correctly functioning, neutral, moving part. It is more important to 'operate', to 'function', to accept one's role, than to live: living is for leisure, which itself is mechanised. The great antithesis, nature, provides the shocks: earthquakes and nightmares.

Earthquake, nightmares – and carnival. We only have to consider the official response to the Notting Hill Carnival to see that it too does not conform, is 'incompetent' and unnecessary. The arguments deployed against it are all totally in the language of the Regulators: crime, cost of policing it, rubbish-collection, disturbance of the peace, no doubt Special Branch overtime costs – the very language of the opposition triumphantly validates the need for the event itself.

Contrast with the two old ladies the five men from Wang with whom I travelled south on a plane more recently: full of lager, loud-laughing, speaking in big voices, they were the new face of competence. Two were English, one Dutch, one Black, one Chinese from Hong Kong – but totally indistinguishable in voice or behaviour. They were brimming with self-confidence, clearly had 'loadsamoney', and spoke of trips to Nanking to instruct the Red Chinese in Wang's uses, and the similar trip they were returning from, to Scotland, which they found a cause for great mirth, commenting that they had not met any nationalists on their trip – a day-trip. One of them, as the plane came down from 35,000 feet, began to suffer very painful sinus problems, a pain racked his skull, he could scarcely talk, his body was tense to breaking with it. The others had only one way to cope – to make loud jokes about it. The air hostess gave him aspirin and water and even she was hurt by their shafts of wit. He then revealed he had a two-hour drive to Hastings in front of him: the others fell silent. They had nothing to offer – pain, inconvenience, did not form part of their world.

Activities below the waist – now industrialised as 'screwing' or 'shafting' – have become fetishised into appendices which have to conform to set patterns within marriage, outside marriage, and which relate to one's business efficiency and status.

All of this is fairly commonplace within the US, which in this as in all things is the Utopia we aspire to. But I think this path is even more dangerous for the English than the mix that is America. Our scarcities and deficiencies have made us bitter, uptight, inclined to self-laceration and guilt, which not many Americans feel about anything. As we go down the narrowing path to the Regulated Corporate State, these characteristics could turn very nasty.

Some form of active response must come from the arts – whether to the political structures, or to the power-structures, or to the psychic perils for even the most triumphal. The most triumphal, of course, can afford their own brand of therapy – squash, country weekends, holidays, shooting stags in the highlands, American Express Goldcard visits to *Les Misérables*, all spoken in the vocal tones within their range, all reinforcing their ideology. From their first lesson, their first playground experiences, their upbringing on all levels, they have had their humanity defined, shaped, to help them grow into conforming, competent people, able to get off aeroplanes quickly and in an orderly manner, even when they're on fire. Perhaps for all our sakes we should be wanting them to break their moulds, or at least pay some respect to the other sounds in the forest, before their horseplay burns it down.

Of the other groups in our society, those with work are even now in danger of either tripping down the primrose path of Eric Hammond into an individualistic dog-eat-dog paradise on the American model, or sinking back into the gruff, punitive grumblings of the old-style union bosses, and clinging to privileges and differentials that enshrine a Victorian capitalist order.

If, ultimately, they are in the Marxist model to be the levers of a social revolution, then they need to be asked to think a great deal more than they are doing, and to expand their consciousness a great deal more too. The fact is that in the accelerating change from labour-intensive to capital-intensive production, the working class has to its shame allowed all the benefits of the application of technology to be appropriated by the capital-owning and the managerial classes. This has been largely achieved by the deluded self-interest of those workers who think their jobs are safe failing to find the way to unite with those under threat in a national, or better international way to socialize the benefits, to use them for the good of society as a whole, rather than small pay-rises for a dwindling number of workers and great increases in wealth to financiers, entrepreneurs, managers and investors. This unity did not happen. There is now a great struggle about to take place for the soul of the working class. The outcome is crucial for our society.

As to the last sector of society, the dispossessed, The Resistance – they are the non-people, the work-shy who have to be kept quiet, orderly and out of the way of the Great Machine. The carnival is above all for them. To form part of an unofficial counter-culture that will enrich lives, raise spirits and prepare the way for the future. Out of the language, the experience, the imagination, the needs of the people, a truly popular art; it can only be judged by its working achievements, but it can be helped along by some thinking and talking – which we have been trying to do.